Producing Fruit or Just Working!

A Primary Study on the
Fruit of the Spirit

by Ralph W. Szasz
Forward by Dr. Robert Lemon

Copyright © 1997 by Ralph W. Szasz

All rights reserved. Written permission must be secured from the publisher to use or reproduce any part of this book, except for brief quotations in critical reviews or articles.

ISBN 1-57502-481-0

King James Bible

New American Standard Bible (NAS.),
Lockman Foundation, La Habra, CA.

The Amplified Bible (AMP.),
Lockman Foundation, La Habra, Ca.

New International Version (NIV.),
International Bible Society

Dake's Annotated Reference Bible (DAKES),
Finis Jennings Dake.

Strong's Concordance (S).

Young's Concordance (Y).

Webster's Encyclopedic Unabridged Dictionary
of the English Language (D),
Dilithium Press Ltd.

Printed in the USA by

MP
MORRIS PUBLISHING

3212 East Highway 30 • Kearney, NE 68847 • 1-800-650-7888

We live in a time of great change in the body of Christ. This book is designed by its author to equip you for the days that lie ahead. We are facing a new millennium. The year 2000 will bring many challenges and it is a solid book like this that will help us deal with these challenges.

After reading this book, I was impressed with the work that has been done. The author has done a great amount of research and I know has studied each point carefully to make this a cutting edge book for such a time as this. So, it is easy for me to recommend this book to you the reader. I believe it will be a blessing to your life.

Dr. Robert H. Lemon

Ralph W. Szasz. A graduate from Kean College, Union, N.J., 1976, and from Rhema Bible Training Centre, Broken Arrow, OK., 1991. Worked as engineering tech to auto sales to janitorial to pizza delivery to support family. Has taught several times, from children to adults, many bible study series, both in classroom setting and from the pulpit. Now embarking into a field in which God has called him. This first book is a first step towards that goal.

Dr. Robert Lemon. Founder and president of Harvest Fire Ministries Inc. and presently senior pastor of Abiding Word Fellowship in Lake City, Mi. In obedience to the apostolic call on his life, he travels in America and foreign countries speaking a prophetic word to the end time church. He is a father to many young pastors, and is highly respected across many denominational borders, and shares from over 37 years of ministerial experience.

Index

1 Introduction: What is Fruit? 1

2 Is it Flesh or is it Spirit? 3

3 Love: The Foundation of The Fruit 7

4 Joy: The First Step on The Foundation of Love 18

5 Peace: The Second Step on The Foundation of Love 26

6 Longsuffering: The Third Step on The Foundation of Love......33

7 Gentleness:: The Fourth Step on The Foundation of Love 40

8 Goodness: The Fifth Step on The Foundation of Love 45

9 Faith: The Sixth Step on The Foundation of Love 51

10 Meekness: The Seventh Step on The Foundation of Love........56

11 Temperance: The Eighth Step on The Foundation of Love 64

12 Conclusion and Summary 72

1

Introduction

One autumn morning, in the northwest hills of New Jersey, a family gets up early with great expectations. Dad promised the family a nice drive in the country through the many picturesque sites of farms and orchards preparing for the winter months ahead. Farmers gathering in the harvest, taking them to the markets to be sold for all their labors. Other farmers gather in the hay and provender for their livestock, in order to feed them through the winter.

The family continues and sees many apple orchards with ripe, juicy, and red apples, ready to be picked. The apples were very alluring, causing the mouths of the entire family to water, greatly yearning just to have one bite. They come to the provided parking lot of this orchard where they saw a sign, "Apples, Apples, Apples...Everyone Loves Apples". This orchard was one of the many along the country lanes where you picked your own. This made the day even more exciting, since they could pick the best for themselves. They went in to the cashier/owner where they bought several baskets to put their apples in. Dad said, "Let's look first and see where the best apples are". Therefore they split up and made a thorough search. They came back together, after a while, to decide where the best was, but they all gave a good report of their findings. Dad decided, to prevent any arguments, they would split up again and just start picking the best from the area each investigated. The baskets soon became full to overflowing with apples, with each having an apple in their mouth. They came and reveled together over their very profitable pickings of superbly appealing good apples, ready for eating, cooking, baking, or canning.

They loaded their car and went back to the cashier/owner to have a talk with him and to ask some questions about how the apples, that he grew were in such abundance and in such seeming perfection. The owner was taken back, since he only gets back complainers. Therefore he invited them to his home and offered refreshments with pastries (apple of course), and proceeded to explain how he took care of his orchard.

He continues, "The trees are prepared in spring and the blossoms come out. The busy bees pollinate, then soon after the blossoms fall off. The weather continues to warm, and the leaves come out with the small apples. The hired workers and I then go out and prune off the non-productive branches, so the producing branches can receive all the nourishing sap to feed the future red, juicy, and ripe apples. When the autumn season comes up, I just open up and let the people in to pick away". Dad, then, asked one more question which seemed ridiculous, yet it was very profound, "Did the trees ever struggle to produce the apples"? The owner chuckled and said, "No, it's in the tree already, to grow apples and does so every year the same. It's the tree's nature to produce apples and it doesn't struggle to do so. It would, if it had to produce oranges". Dad, then satisfied, left and went home after a very productive day.

This short illustrative story shows that the fruit is what the people are looking for, so they can enjoy the partaking of it. The tree has in it the nature to produce apples. When we decide to receive Jesus as our Savior and Lord, God puts in us the nature of the fruit of the Spirit. When we decide to release our faith, like sap in the tree, then we will start developing the fruit. We do this by daily feeding on God's word, which increases our faith and causes our fruit to grow. The apples ripened and became appealing and alluring, but our "better fruit" will offer more, better than temporary satisfaction, to a hungry world. We need to notice that the tree didn't produce fruit for itself but for others to enjoy. We also must produce fruit for others to enjoy and benefit from. Jesus said in Matthew 10:8, "...freely you received, freely give". Jesus expounded to the apostles, that the given ability to heal the sick, raise the dead, cleanse the leper, and cast out demons, was not for them alone, but must be offered to minister to others, the fruit of their given abilities. This way, the needed satisfaction of the fruit of healing, raising, cleansing, and casting out, can be obtained by the one who needed it and not the apostles' own satisfaction.

2

Is it flesh or is it spirit?

Let us look at the book of Galatians, chapter 5. We will notice in this chapter, that Paul was expounding on our dual nature. When we receive Jesus as Savior and Lord, our spirit man became a new creation, totally compatible to God. Our flesh bodies and souls (our will, emotion, and intellect) did not change. Therefore it is still in opposition or rebellion towards God. What do we do in this situation, for it looks like a dilemma? We have to discover what our new nature is, within our spirit, and how we can tap into it, so that we can act accordingly to please God. We need to see, that with our old nature, we were always self-serving. Even when we were helping others, we looked for some kind of self-gratification for all of our actions.

The proof is, when I asked scores of people if they were going to heaven, they responded, "Probably, since my good deeds outweigh my bad deeds". They have the idea, that even the good deeds are measured as a merit for personal gain. These superficial actions, many times, lead to hurting others, when the desired end does not come together as wanted. We Christians do the same thing because we have not fully understood for ourselves what this salvation (to bring back to the original intended state of complete wholeness) means, and was received as a gift by grace through faith. Therefore, there is the same kind of fighting and bickering between us Christians. It says in **Galatians 5:15, "But if you bite and devour one another, take care lest you be consumed by one another". NASB.** This can be stopped only when, in **Galatians 5:16, "But I say, walk by the Spirit, and you will not carry out the desire of the flesh". NASB.**

We need to understand, that this situation, in our dual nature, can produce nothing but real problems. God didn't leave us in this situation however, without showing how we can be above our fleshly ways of the past and start progressing forward in this new life. This new way of living is shown in **Galatians 5:18, "If you are led by the Spirit, you**

are not under the law". NASB. When we decide to allow God to lead us through this life, then the dictates of the law, which only incites the flesh to rebel against it, will not lord it over us and make us subject to it.

Let's look in Galatians 5, verses 19 to 21, which shows us the works of the flesh. We will notice, that the flesh can only follow after the works. Therefore, no matter how much works we do, we can't ever meet the expectations of pleasing God. God is never moved by our works, because by the works alone, it always comes from the root of self-serving or self-gratifying intentions.

Verses 19 to 21 lists the major works of the flesh and they are manifest. Reference sources are used to explain: The Strong's Concordance (S), and the dictionary (D). *Manifest is (S): "shine out, apparent, public and external", and is (D): "to prove and put beyond doubt and question".*

There are 17 listed in this scripture and we will explore it for a short while, so that we can understand and not be mistaken by deceit.

1. Adultery: (D) voluntary (not forced on us) sexual intercourse between a married person and someone other than his or her lawful spouse.
2. Fornication: (S) harlotry (adultery and incest) and idolatry. (D) voluntary sexual intercourse between two unmarried persons or two persons not married to each other.
3. Uncleanness: (S) the quality of physical and moral impurity, lewd. (D) morally impure, evil, vile. Having physical or moral blemish so as to make impure according to the laws.
4. Lasciviousness: (S) not continent, licentiousness (sexually unrestrained, going beyond customary or proper bounds and limits) including vices. (D) inclined to lustfulness, wanton, lewd, arousing sexual desire.
5. Idolatry: (S) image-worship. (D) excessive or blind adoration, reverence or devotion of any person or thing that is not God.
6. Witchcraft: (S) medication (pharmacy), by extension magic (charm, remedy). (D) the art or practices of a witch; sorcery; magic. We need to see that witchcraft is of the flesh, therefore we need not be afraid of it, but overcome it by standing up against it through the word of God.
7. Hatred: (S) hostility by implication a reason for opposition. (D) intense dislike or extreme aversion or hostility (animosity).
8. Variance: (S) quarrel by implication wrangling. (D) disagreement, dispute, or quarrel. Official permit to do something normally forbidden by regulations.

Is it flesh or is it spirit?

9. Emulation: (S) properly "heat", zeal in an unfavorable one, jealousy, malice. (D) effort or desire to equal or excel others, jealous rivalry.
10. Wrath: (S) passion as if breathing hard, fierceness, indignation. (D) strong, stern, or fierce anger, deeply resentful indignation, ire.
11. Strife: (S) properly intrigue (to beguile by appeal to the curiosity, fancy, or interest...to plot craftily or use underhand machinations), by implication faction. (D) vigorous or bitter conflict, discord, or antagonism.
12. Seditions: (S) disunion, dissertion. (D) incitement of discontent, or rebellion against a government; rebellious disorder.
13. Heresies: (S) properly a choice, specially a party (opinion), abstractly disunion. (D) opinion or doctrine at variance with orthodox or accepted doctrine; and act of choosing.
14. Envyings: (S) ill-willed (as detraction) that is jealousy (spite). (D) the feeling of discontent or jealousy usually with ill-will at seeing another's superiority, advantages, or success.
15. Murders: (S) to slay, murder. (D) the unlawful killing of another human creature with malice aforethought.
16. Drunkenness: (S) an intoxicant that is by implication intoxication (to heat, sweeten, and spice). (D) pertaining to, proceeding from, or marked by intoxication.
17. Revellings: (S) a carousel as if letting loose. (D) indulging in boisterous festivities; to raise tumult.

We have now gone through this list of the works of the flesh, and can see that these actions originate from the fleshly natural desires. They are from the flesh and not the spirit, therefore we are not to fear them. These cannot overpower or force us to do them, because the flesh part of us is not the strongest, when we are born-again. It is not to say that we will not have to fight to keep the flesh under control, but we can be fully assured we will win, if we do not give up acting accordingly, on the word of God. The Word of God always gives us the right direction to go, which leads to ultimate victory!

It states in **I Corinthians 10:13: "No temptation has overtaken you but such as is common to man; and God is faithful, who will not allow you to be tempted beyond what you are able, but with the temptation will provide the way of escape also, that you may be able to endure it". NASB.** The most common thing among men is his fleshly nature. If one fighter lifts up his opponent over his head, the opponent can no longer fight, and usually is called the loser. God has given to us the ability to overcome the fleshly originated temptation. We need to find out what this ability of overcoming is and how to use it. The tree produces the fruit after its kind, therefore we are to do the same by producing the fruit of the nature of God in us. This nature was placed in us when we were born-again, by receiving the benefits of the redemptive work of Jesus on the cross and His resurrection.

This nature is best described as the "Fruit of the Spirit", found in **Galatians 5:22-23: "But the fruit of the Spirit is love, joy, peace, longsuffering, gentleness, goodness, faith, meekness, temperance: against such there is no law". KJV.**

We should notice that the word "fruit" is singular and not fruits plural. We must conclude that the nine parts are included in the one result of fruit. The apple has many parts to make one apple, likewise the nine parts comprise the one fruit. Therefore, we must also conclude that the nine parts or functions need to be working together, because we should benefit from the whole fruit. *The word fruit is defined (S): "fruit as plucked (seized)".* This means that the fruit must be fully ripe to be useful, or to be plucked or seized. All the parts must be mature fully to be useful. The apple, for example, must be mature or ripe for consumption, and have seeds to produce the next generation of trees. Therefore, we need to strive to become fully mature in the fruit of the Spirit, to obtain the full benefits of the nature of God within us.

3

Love: the foundation of the fruit of the Spirit

We have discovered, in the previous chapter, that the fruit of the Spirit was put into us when we accepted and received Jesus as our Lord and Savior, through the redemptive work of His, by the death on the cross and His resurrection. We also discovered that the fruit was comprised of nine parts or functions. These nine parts must work together to obtain the full benefits. This growth gained is by our full co-operation of working in the nine parts or functions.

The first part of the fruit is called love. The word love, in the English language, covers a multitude of definitions. It can cover an affection for another creature, like a pet, or liking an object, like a car or house, or a great pleasure, like music or dancing, or affection for others well-being, like children or neighbors. It also covers having a profound tender and passionate affection for the opposite sex. Even tennis uses love in its scoring. It can get very confusing, needless to say, to what the word love can mean, since it has different meanings and shades to its descriptions. Love, with all these meanings, still doesn't describe what it really is, as God sees it. All of the previous meanings only describe what will be satisfying to our fleshly nature, and how we can obtain the benefit. If we work from this standpoint, we will never get into position to start laying the foundation for developing the fruit of the Spirit. God always looks at things from the spiritual point of view, therefore we can continue to learn how God works. God will always come from the spirit, so that it will never fail. I have never seen God fail, therefore if we come from the point of the spirit, we will also never fail.

Let us look at the word love from a biblical prospective. *The word love is translated from the Greek word "agape", which means benevolence or affection (S). Benevolence means (D): desire to do good to others; good-will; charitableness.* It, in other words, is a willful giving of oneself to another to meet the real need. *Affection means (D): a fond attachment, devotion or love; an act of influencing or acting upon*, in other words, a love that comes from the heart for another where we personally are involved, therefore being an influence to the person and acting upon the need to help them overcome.

A God kind of love always comes from the heart or spirit and doesn't originate from the flesh or emotion. The love the world demonstrates is always determined greatly by the circumstances and situations in life. When the fleshly or emotional love is satisfied, it stops working. God's kind of love is always steadfast, even when the circumstances and situations are not. This kind of love is best demonstrated by Scripture found in **I Corinthians 13: 4-8a: (KJV)**

"Charity suffereth long, and is kind; charity envyeth not; charity vaunteth not itself, is not puffed up, doth not behave itself unseemly, seeketh not her own, is not easily provoked, thinketh no evil; rejoiceth not in iniquity, but rejoiceth in the truth; beareth all things, believeth all things, hopeth all things, endureth all things. Charity never faileth..."

We can see that this can be a very tall order to follow. All these things comprise the function of love that God has put in us believers, therefore we can reach out to the real needs of others. God has put this love in us, therefore do we not think that God has put in us the ability also to use this love effectively? God never commands us to do something without giving us the ability to carry it out, otherwise God would not be just in asking us to do them. Let us examine each phrase in this Scripture to learn how they function and how to implement them in our lives.

The first phrase is "charity suffereth long", and described (S): "to be long spirited, that is (objectively) forbearing, or (subjectively) patient...to be with long enduring temper, that is leniently".

Charity or giving love is long spirited, and stays alive long after all others give up. When pressures come against us operating in this love, we won't give up, but keep on going. Ever notice that a high spirited person is rarely down, depressed, or despondent with life? This is how we, operating in love, should act. We never let the situation get us down, but we look for the opportunity within the problem, becoming an asset or help and not a liability. How can we help others when we are overcome by their problems? No matter what the situation others are experiencing, we must objectively forebear the faults of others. We must not dwell on the faults but forebear, giving us the opportunity to perceive in how to help others out of the situation. Consequently, we subjectively are patient with others, giving them time to adjust and learn how to come out. We, with longsuffering even temper, that is leniency, can work together with them to finally become self-sufficient.

Love: the foundation of the fruit of the Spirit

Some believers have very short patience with others, which leads to condemning them because they don't respond as expected. They may be struggling with sin, which may seem like they will never overcome or conquer. When they are condemned or given up on, they will feel totally defeated and will not care any longer.

We should be helping others in love by patiently working with them, even if it takes seemingly forever. When they finally overcome, the reward will outweigh the effort put in. If they never intend to change, we must back off and earnestly pray for them, thereby not pushing them away permanently. God, by this, can send another person that will help motivate them to want to change. This action also includes patience.

Next, charity or giving love is "kind", and is described (S): "the one who shows himself useful, that is acting benevolently. He is employed, that is by implication useful, in manner or morals and he looks for ways to furnish what is needed".

Most of us have a misguided view of what to be "kind" really means. We think of a mild mannered and gentle person, having no standards, just drifting along never affecting anyone. Yet the dictionary describes "kind": "a good or benevolent nature or disposition, being indulgent, considerate and helpful". Therefore we know, that to be kind, is a very powerful aspect of love. Love is very active and not static.

We have seen people who are always looking for ways to help others. They keep reaching out, in other words, a real people person. An example is a grocery clerk that lends a helping hand in finding items for shoppers or taking the groceries out to the car, making it more convenient for the shopper.

These are the things that describe a "kind" person. They do not say "it is not my job", but make themselves useful in whatever situation there may be. When we look for them, they are employed in some work, making it easier, even before the problem arise, and are prepared and ready to help, being useful.

We may not know what we need, yet this person is ready to furnish what is needed, therefore eliminating confusion. It is not difficult to love people, even in very stressful situations, when we act this way. Our goal is to be useful in furnishing what is needed and not satisfying ourselves.

This same thing is illustrated in Scripture found in **I John 3:17-18: "But whoever has the world's goods, and beholds his brother in need and closes his heart against him, how does the love of God abide in him? Little children, let us not love with word or with tongue, but in deed and truth.".** NASB

When we operate in love, we will know we are kind, by reaching out to others, and being useful and furnishing what is needed. If we close our hearts against them, we cut off the love and the benefits derived from it. We will discover more and more, that love always reaches out to others, as we delve further into love.

The third point is that "charity (giving love) envieth not". The word "envieth" is described (S): "to have warmeth of feeling against; in the proper sense as heat, that is figuratively zeal (in an unfavorable one, jealousy or an emnity, malice)", and (D): "a feeling of discontent or jealousy usually with ill-will at seeing anothers' superiority, advantages or success". **An alternate version: "boils over with jealousy". AMP.**

There are people who really love us to fail. They never intend to amount to any thing in this life, therefore they don't want their apple cart, so to speak, to be disrupted. When they see someone succeed they develop a warmth of feeling against them. They allow themselves (not the devil, not God, and not the one they are against), to fester in this, setting in motion a boiling inside with deep anger and jealousy. They devise evil schemings, trying to overthrow the one succeeding. All this really leads them to is failure on their part, even though they may temporarily slow down the one succeeding.

When we wholeheartedly decide to love God's way, we want and desire others to succeed. We will go out of our way to help and not feel inferior because of the superiority, advantage or success of others. Our lives are not pulled down because of the success of others, therefore we can help and possibly learn from them and add to our success also.

The fourth part is "charity (giving love) vaunteth not itself". "Vaunteth" is described (S): "a braggart or to boast or brag on oneself", and (D): "to speak vaingloriously of oneself".

There are those who vaingloriously expound their miniscule achievements or take credit for the work done by others. They speak highly of themselves by putting others down, and brag on the achievements of others as their own. They take the credit and cover up the evidence, so that the real person who did the work, doesn't receive the credit.

When I worked as an engineering tech, the engineer I worked for, would take all the credit for the projects created. Practically all the engineering designs needed to be redesigned in order for them to work, and he would chew me out for the redesign. When he found them to work past his expectations, he would run and brag on how he made them work better than expected, never giving me the credit. He wasn't a Christian, therefore he couldn't act in Bible love, yet many Christians do the same, even to the expense of their name and honor. We know that Bible love doesn't focus on our achievements by putting others down, but by reaching out to pull others up.

Love: the foundation of the fruit of the Spirit

The next phrase on charity (giving love) is "not puffed up". It is defined (S): "to be inflated, that is figuratively make proud or haughty"', and (Y): "a commendation, especially an exaggeration", and (D): "an exaggerated praise, especially when given for selfish motives".

Those who vaunt themselves, take credit from other's achievements and brags about it. Those who puff themselves up, do legitimately achieve something of importance, yet they actually become arrogant about it.

We know, in sales, there are difficult salesmen and customers. I remember a particular salesman, who puffed himself up on how he would sell to difficult customers, by trying to confuse them during the negotiations. He may have gotten some sales, yet he never developed trust. True salesmen learn to value customers (a form of love) and will do the best to ensure customer satisfaction and repeat business.

We, as Christians, must learn to value a soul highly, so that we can love them. Our part is to ensure that this soul sees our love in action, possibly leading them to the saving knowledge of Jesus. We, as true soul winners, must not get inflated, proud, or haughty on how many souls we lead to Jesus. We, simply, love them and let the Holy Spirit do the rest.

The next phrase on charity (giving love) is "doth not behave itself unseemly". It is defined (S): "to be, that is act unbecomingly", and (D): "not in keeping with established standards of tastes or proper form; unbecoming or undignified in appearance; improper in speech, conduct, etc...". **An alternate version: "it is not rude (unmannerly) and does not act unbecomingly". AMP.**

Employers must guard against acting very foolishly. Lambasting employees, because of missed criteria, is totally unnecessary and not in keeping with established standards of taste or proper form. They, when venting anger, do not understand why employees do not respond and just quit their jobs. When dressing down the employee, they are undignified in appearance to them, therefore losing all respect. Employers will go a lot further if they would keep their cool and help the employee overcome the problem. If the employee is irresponsible, the employer can relieve the employee without losing his respect.

I heard, one time, a preacher say when he went to lunch, how he became embarrassed by his associate's actions. This man, during the lunch rush, would frequently blurt out loud, "Bless God" or "Praise the Lord", disrupting everyone's lunch. When his meal was served he prayed so loud that everyone thought he was a jerk. The people were right to think that way, for we Christians should not become spectacles, trying to convince that we believe in God.

There is a world of difference between boldness and rudeness. Love always attains to achieve harmony between us giving and they receiving.

We must act becomingly, keeping with the established standards of taste and proper form, where they can see that the love administered is genuine. God's love always reaches out to help others, and doesn't overimpress by being loud, rude and unbecoming.

Charity or giving love is "seeketh not her own" and is defined (S): "to seek (literally or figuratively); (specifically in a bad sense to plot against life. This seeking implies a search for something hidden, or to desire, require or question)", and (D): "to try to obtain". **An alternate version: "doesn't insist on its own rights or its own ways, for it is not selfseeking". AMP**

Many times people who start to advance in skills, forget that others have already attained them. They barge in and order others around, causing confusion and a drop in production. When we insist on our own way, we won't listen to alternatives already in place. We must not be self-seeking, for it will frustrate us, leading us to where we want to harass others.

We now know that self-seeking is not operating in love, for love doesn't seek, desire or require for itself. True Bible love seeks a way to help reach out to others to help overcome their problems, giving them the opportunity to see the victory.

Charity or giving love "is not easily provoked". "Provoked" is described (S): "to sharpen alongside, that is figuratively, to exasperate", and (D): "to anger, enrage, exasperate or vex", in other words, "to irritate to a high degree; annoy extremely; infuriate". **An alternate version: "it is not touchy or fretful or resentful". AMP.**

People controlled by circumstances are very easily provoked. They have the attitude that others come to cause them harm, and allow themselves to be cut emotionally or spiritually by the words or actions of others. When they permit this to continue, the cuts get even deeper and sharper, and the sharpening alongside or exasperation builds up, where their thinking and attitude is no longer valid. Therefore, they become touchy, fretful and resentful, where no one can approach them to help.

True Bible love never allows the situation to dictate how we should respond. We must look for the opportunity to reach out, in every situation, to solve them, whether for ourselves or for others. We must not allow, whether emotionally or spiritually, the situation to cut into us, where we start looking inward, to pity ourselves, but to look outwardly to help others find and reach their desired goal.

Love always reaches out, just like God reaches out to us, through His Son Jesus Christ. When we decide to accept His reaching out to us, He meets our real need, which is life with God. This includes everything we need to live life richly.

We proceed on, with charity or giving love "thinketh no evil", described (S): "to take an inventory, that is estimate whether literally

Love: the foundation of the fruit of the Spirit

or figuratively", and (D): "to meditate; ponder; analyze or examine with the intellect, as to reach a decision or conclusion...to bear in mind, recollect or remember...to have in mind, as a plan, intent or purpose". An alternate version: "it takes no account of the evil done to it (it pays no attention to the suffered wrong)". AMP.

We have met people that can tell us in detail what happened to them many years ago. They nurse constantly the situation, mulling over it, going to the extent of remembering every detail. Sometimes it doesn't satisfy their hurt or lack, therefore they add to it making it more grandiose. They take a detailed account of everything, inventorying the situation where they can never forget it. Their mental exercises of meditating, pondering, analyzing and examining, ever looking to reach a decision or conclusion, but never apprehending because they cannot change the past. They look so much into the past, that they cannot see into the future where they see themselves free from the situation.

Paul says in **Philippians 3:13-14: "Brothers, I do not consider myself yet to have taken hold of it. But one thing I do: Forgetting what is behind and straining toward what is ahead, I press on toward the goal to win the prize for which God has called me heavenward in Christ Jesus".** NIV. We see here, that love always reaches out to help by straining toward what is ahead. Love is not bogged down by the past, but is straining toward what is ahead in solved problems and situations. People are bogged down already and need not be reminded, instead need to strain toward what is ahead, where their problems are solved and themselves free from it, just like God provides in His salvation for mankind.

Charity or giving love "Rejoiceth not in iniquity, but rejoiceth in the truth". The first "rejoiceth" is described (S): "cheerful, that is a calmly happy or well-off attitude", in other words, it doesn't pleasure in iniquity. "Iniquity" is described (S): legal injustice (properly the quality, by implication the act); moral wrongfulness (of character, life or act)"

The following Scriptures describe the opposite to what the first phrase states: **Psalms 10:3: "He boasts of the cravings of his heart; he blesses the greedy and reviles the Lord", Romans 1:32: "Although they know God's righteous decree that those who do such things deserve death, they not only continue to do these very things but also approve of those who practice them"' Psalms 50:18: "When you see a thief, you join with him; you throw in your lot with adulterers", Hosea 7:3: "They delight the king with their wickedness, the princes with their lies".** NIV

The second "rejoiceth" is described (S): "to sympathize in gladness and congratulation in and with the truth (in doctrine and profession)".

The following Scriptures describes what the second phrase states: **2 John 1:4: "It has given me great joy to find some of your children walking in the truth, just as the Father commanded us", 3 John 1:3: "It gave me great joy to have some brothers come and tell about your faithfulness to the truth and how you continue to walk in the truth". NIV** The Word of God is the truth as expressed in **Jeremiah 15:16: "When your words came, I ate them; they were my joy and my heart's delight, for I bear your name, O Lord God Almighty". NIV.**

Charity or giving love "beareth all things", where "beareth" is described (S): "to roof over, that is figuratively to cover with silence (endure patiently)", in other words, "protects" NIV, and (D): "to be patient or self-controlled when subject to annoyance or provocation".

We, Born-again believers, are at different levels spiritually, and have different ways of thinking and acting, therefore we must not despise others who haven't attained to our level of maturity, even if they are believers longer than we have been. We must avoid at all costs the "holier than thou" attitude, which causes the unbelievers to despise this life offered by God to all men. Believers will also shrink back from growing spiritually and give up on trying to attain a life of victory with God, but instead they settle for a life of defeat and despair.

These Scriptures add to on how love "beareth all things/protects". **Proverbs 17:9: "He who covers over an offense promotes love, but whoever repeats the matter separates close friends", Romans 15:1: "We who are strong ought to bear with the failings of the weak and not please ourselves", Galatians 6:1-2: "Brothers, if someone is caught in a sin, you who are spiritual should restore him gently, But watch yourself, or you also may be tempted. Carry each other's burdens, and in this way you will fulfill the law of Christ", I Peter 4:8: "Above all, love each other deeply, because love covers over a multitude of sins". NIV.**

True Bible love does not excuse sin and error, yet does not broadcast it all over. Love covers with silence by going to the person involved to help bring them out and restore them. We must continually help people overcome their problems and situations and keep strict confidence by not telling others to betray them. God, in His ultimate has provided us love, where we have the ability to cover with silence their faults, therefore we can go over to them and truly help them overcome.

Charity or giving love "believeth all things", is defined (S): "to have faith (in, upon, or with respect to a person or thing), that is credit; by implication to entrust (especially one's spiritual well-being to Christ)", and (D): "to have confidence in the truth, the existence or

Love: the foundation of the fruit of the Spirit

the reliability of something, although without absolute proof that one is right in doing so". **An alternate version: "...is ever ready to believe the best of everyone". AMP.**

We believers have positive hope in life and see things from a Godly prospective. We do not search for the bad but the best in others to help them see that they are not beyond hope of ever coming out of their situation. We must act, by having faith in, upon or respect to the person or thing, thereby creating trust and credibility, where they see our genuine outreach to them, because we believe in them. They will, by this, have a better outlook on life, and start helping themselves come out on top victoriously.

These Scripture will help understand how love "believeth all things". **Galatians 5:6: "For in Christ Jesus neither circumcision nor uncircumcision has any value. (in other words, religious acts don't cut it) The only thing that counts is faith (believing) expressing itself in love", James 2:17: "In the same way, faith (believing) by itself, if it is not accompanied by action, is dead", I John 5:4: "...for everyone born of God overcomes the world. This is the victory that has overcome the world, even our faith (believing)". NIV.**

Believing is always accompanied by actions and motivated by charity or giving love, and not by religious acts imposed on people. We believers demonstrate our believing or faith in others by showing them a better way. People overcome by their problems or situations, must be shown that they do not have to be. God has provided a way out, through the redemptive work of Jesus, making us victorious already.

Charity or giving love "hopeth all things", is described (S): "to expect or confide", and (D): "to place trust in or rely on; to look for with reason of justification". **An alternate version: "its hopes are fadeless under all circumstances". AMP.**

There is nothing that is absolutely hopeless with God. Two Scriptures back this: **Mark 10:27: "Jesus looked at them and said, 'With man this is impossible, but not with God; all things are possible with God'", and Luke 18:27: "Jesus replied, 'What is impossible with men is possible with God'". NIV.**

We see that with God there is always hope, and we never have to feel doomed to the circumstances of life. Therefore we can show others to see this for themselves coming out victoriously, over their circumstances.

Here are some Scriptural references describing Biblical hope: **Romans 4:18: "Against all hope, Abraham in hope believed and so became the father of many nations just as it had been said to him...".** Abraham continued in hope, in spite of his old age, or

Sarah's old age and barreness. **Romans 5:5: "And hope does not disappoint us, because God has poured out his love into our hearts by the Holy Spirit, whom he has given us".** We know that we have hope from God, therefore we can reach out to others, and have them come to understand the same. **I Peter 3:15: "...Always be prepared to give an answer to everyone who asks you to give the reason for the hope that you have". I John 3:3: "Everyone who has this hope in him purifies himself, just as he is pure". NIV.**

We have this hope inside us already, when born-again. Therefore, there is no need to be fretting over any situation because this hope residing in us helps us to overcome.

Charity or giving love "endureth all things" is defined (S): *"to stay under (behind), that is remain; figuratively to undergo, that is bear (trials), have fortitude, persevere", in other words, to stay under in a given place, state, relation or expectancy, and (D): "to support adverse force or influence of any kind; suffer without yielding".* **An alternate version: "it endures everything (without weakening)". AMP.**

The love that God gave us abides in our hearts where we put it into operation to help others, reaching out to them. We must stand steadfast, in love, because the pressures that come against us can cause us to weaken. When helping others, we must not get overly involved and get trapped in the problem they are experiencing, but look at the whole picture and discover the root of the problem! Love, which sometimes may seem harsh, doesn't look to satisfy the wishes of others but to resolve the problem.

Here are some Scriptural references describing Biblical endurance/steadfastness: **John 15:9-10: "As the Father has loved me, so have I loved you. Now remain in my love. If you obey my commands, you will remain in my love, just as I have obeyed my Father's commands and remain in his love".** Jesus had to endure, in spite of all the persecutions against Him as He ministered to the people by His Father's commands. **Romans 2:7: "To those who by persistence in doing good seek glory (Substance and integrity), honor (honesty, integrity and truth) and immortality, he will give eternal life".** There is a real reward in doing good. **Galatians 6:9: "Let us not become weary in doing good, for at the proper time we will reap a harvest if we do not give up". Hebrews 12:1b: "...let us throw off everything that hinders (problems, situations and adversities) and the sin (the mistakes and errors, whether willing or not) that so easily entangles, and let us run with perseverance the race marked out for us". NIV.** We can always endure without caving in, with God's kind of love.

Love: the foundation of the fruit of the Spirit

Charity or giving love never "faileth", is defined (S): "to drop away; specifically, be driven out of one's course; figuratively, to lose, become inefficient", and (D): "to be or become deficient or lacking; to be unsuccessful in the performance or completion of", **An alternate version: "(never fades out of becomes obsolete or comes to an end)". AMP.**

True Biblical love can never fail, because its source is from God which never ends, therefore we can always depend on it to see us through. When we decide to stay in the limitless source obtained through love, our course cannot be pushed out of the way. We, then, can help others, knowing that we will never fall short of overcoming the situation.

We have attempted to demonstrate the importance of building a strong foundation of love before pressing on, because without a strong foundation of love the rest of the fruit of the Spirit cannot develop correctly and effectively. The best way to find how love operates most effectively is to study the life of Jesus in the four Gospels and discover that love always made Him victorious in every situation, whether good or bad.

4

Joy: the first step on the foundation of love

We have concluded in the previous chapter, the first function of the fruit of the Spirit called love. Love is always reaching out to others to meet the real needs, and is not self-serving. Love has a very strong position and a strong foundation. The foundation of love must operate properly, so that the other eight functions of the fruit of the Spirit can operate properly.

The next function of the fruit of the Spirit, "joy", is defined (S): "cheerfulness, that is calm delight or calmly happy or well off", and (D): "the emotion of great delight or happiness caused by something good or satisfying; keen (characterized by strength and distinctness of perception) pleasure".

Joy is much more than feelings, instead it has a deep rooted character of strength and distinctness of perception where it will last under pressure or scrutiny, unlike superficial feelings. The Bible clearly shows to us the many aspects of joy, therefore when it becomes a reality in us, we will never settle for feelings only.

The first Scripture is found in **Nehemiah 8:10: "...Do not grieve, for the joy of the Lord is your strength".** "Joy" is defined (S): "rejoicing", (to joy again and again continually). This implies that joy should not and must not be affected by outside problems, because joy must come from within us and not from the outside. "Strength" is defined (S): "a fortified place; figuratively a defense".

Joy is a fortified place (stronghold), a defense against the influences by outside problems, therefore, worry/grief is no longer allowed in our lives.

The previous phrase of Scripture states: "do not grieve". "Grieve" is defined (S): "to carve, that is fabricate or fashion; hence (in a bad sense) to worry, pain or anger".

When we worry, pain or anger, it starts carving against us which leaves wounds and scars. If left unattended, it will start fabricating or fash-

Joy: the first step on the foundation of love

ioning our thoughts on things that are not conducive, where our imagination can run wild on supposed negative situations, making them more real than the solution of coming out of it.

We must stay in joy constantly, where we can be fortified and defended against the negative influences of the situations. We will, by this, not become a war casualty, suffering wounds and scars, but living in victory through joy.

Another Scripture is **Ezra 6:16b: "...celebrated the dedication of the house of God with joy".** When we decide to live in joy, celebration is at hand. God did not give us joy and not be able to celebrate any and all occasions for living. When we celebrate with joy, the outside influences cannot enter in and disrupt our lives, because our celebration is in the fact that we are in a fortified place and a defense.

Matthew 2:10 states: "When they (Magi) saw the star, they were overjoyed". The word "overjoyed" is defined (S): "vehemently, that is in a high degree". An alternate version: "thrilled with ecstatic joy". NIV.

We see that the Magi, after their long trip, finally coming to their destination, would be overjoyed! This produced in them the ability to prosper and to gain health and vitality in themselves to continue on, until they found Jesus. Joy will rejuvenate to continue and finish the course laid out for us, knowing that there is a fortified place and a defense keeping us.

Matthew 13:44 states: "The kingdom of heaven is like treasure hidden in a field. When a man found it, he hid it again, and then in his joy went and sold all he had and bought that field". NIV.

We see here that a man found treasure of great value, just like Jesus found in man. This man did not tell everyone but hid it, just like Jesus did by keeping the plan of salvation hidden for us from Satan. This man had joy, which is cheerfulness, that is a calm delight and keen pleasure characterized by strength and distinctness of perception, and was sure of himself being fortified and in a defense, where he sold everything he had and bought it. Jesus, likewise, did the same when He laid down His life and bought back man.

We, with joy, can accomplish whatever God has asked us to do, knowing that we are strengthened behind a protective fortified place and a defense. We can now lay down our lives to the service of God, because we have obtained the treasure God has hidden for us and not from us.

Luke 8:13 states: "Those on the rock are the ones who receive the word with joy when they hear it, but they have no root. They believe for a while, but in the time of testing they fall away". NIV.

We have joy produced in us through the word of God. The difference is that we must develop it to the point where long, deep and strong roots lished, and that we believe it with our whole being. Therefore, when the pressures or temptations come, we will not forgo the joy, but rely on its fortified place and a defense.

Luke 24:41a states: "And while they still did not believe it because of joy and amazement". NIV. *"Still did not believe" is defined (S): "to be unbelieving, that is transitive disbelieve, or by implication to disobey", and (Y): "to be without trust"*

The disciples decided not to believe to the point of disobedience, even though Jesus showed the evidence of His hands and feet. When we read the word of God, which is the evidence to us, we must decide to believe it, whether we understand or not on how it really works, therefore not drifting into willful disobedience.

The word "because" is defined (S): "off, that is away from something near", in other words, (D): "separation, departure, cessation or reversal", and "in place of; instead of".

The disciples allowed their unbelief to take the place of joy that they should of held onto. We, Christians today, must not allow ourselves to continue in unbelief, which always leads to disobedience, therefore never realizing the benefits of joy, but take on belief in order for joy to strengthen us continually.

The word "amazement" is defined (S): "to wonder; by implication to admire", in other words, (D): "to look closely at and be astonished, to gaze with wide opened eyes as at something remarkable and marvelous".

The disciples were told that Jesus would return, yet their unbelief caused them to refuse the truth and be amazed at the sight as if it was not happening. Jesus had to rebuke them.

Joy stabilizes and strengthens us, to give us the confidence to believe the word of God and not to be amazed if it can be true. The strengthening of joy develops commitment in our lives, knowing we can be assured of protection.

John 15:11 states: "I have told you this so that my joy may be in you and that your joy may be complete". *The word "be" is defined (S): "to stay (in a given place, state, relation or expectancy)", and (D): "to continue in the same state; continue to be as specified".*

God gave joy to us and fully expects it to stay with us and in us. Joy must continue in the given place, state, relation or expectancy. The given place is in our hearts to keep us strengthened. The given state is, that it keeps flowing in our lives and stay more alive to us than the problems. The given relation is, that we keep in communication with God, thereby knowing what joy can do for us in times of trouble. The given expectancy is, that we hope or earnestly expect the joy in us to protect us against any adversity.

Joy: the first step on the foundation of love

The joy of Jesus will continue in us, provided we take a decisive step to hold onto it. Should we not think, that anything from Jesus has great value? Therefore, we have the responsibility to appropriate it for ourselves.

The second word "complete" is defined (S): "to make replete, that is literally to cram (a net), level up (a hallow) or figuratively to furnish (imbue, diffuse, influence, satisfy, execute (an office), finish (a period or task)", and (D): "containing all that can be held, filled to the capacity".

God gave joy and fully expects us to develop it in our lives until we are complete in it, that is replete or abundantly supplied. We should be crammed with joy without gaps, leveled up where we won't lack in anything. Joy furnishes the strength we need, in other words, it imbues or impregnates the strength in us. Joy diffuses or spreads out into all areas of our lives and has influence on all we do. We get satisfaction from within ourselves, as joy develops more and more. We can execute, with this joy, an office, or finish a period or task assigned to us, without fear of adversity, for it is a fortified place and a defense. Therefore, we can do what needs to be done, without failing in adversity. Joy comes from Jesus, and if we are determined to work it, joy will not become unfruitful in our lives, because whatever comes from Jesus cannot ever fail.

John 16:20-24 states: "I tell you the truth, you will weep and mourn while the world rejoices. You will grieve, but your grief will turn to joy. A woman giving birth to a child has pain because her time has come; but when her baby is born she forgets the anguish because of her joy that a child is born into the world. So with you: Now is your time of grief, but I will see you again and you will rejoice, and no one will take away your joy. In that day you will no longer ask me anything. I tell you the truth, my Father will give you whatever you ask in my name. Until now you have not asked for anything in my name. Ask and you will receive, and your joy will be complete". NIV.

The words "grieve and grief" are defined (S): "to distress; reflex or pass to be sad or sadness", and (D): "distress caused by loss, affliction, disappointment, etc; grief, sadness or regret".

Jesus foretold to the disciples their grief caused by loss- Him dying on the cross. We must understand, the disciples were looking forward in making Jesus king and to overthrow the Roman oppression.

The word "turn" is defined (S): "to cause to be (generate), that is (reflective) to become (come into being)", and (D): "to change or convert".

God has already provided the remedy or answer for us, therefore when we yield, we can turn from our problems or adversities to Him. God seeks to cause joy to be generated or come into being and to turn around our misguided lives. He desires to create in us the joy needed to empower us.

The word "pain" is defined (S): "to pressure; to crowd", and (D): "excruciating or acute pain, suffering or distress".

Jesus is stating here that when the woman has given birth, all the previous pressures, pain, suffering or distress are forgotten, just like when joy comes into our lives. Joy overpowers the previous pressure, pain, suffering or distress of the problem or adversity, and causes us to be strengthened in a fortified place and a defense, which is this joy.

The word "take" is defined (S): "to lift; by implication to take up or away; figuratively to raise (the voice), keep in suspense (the mind)", and (D): "to get into one's hands, possession, control, etc., by force or artifice".

God's joy is a viable force to be reckoned with. Once we fully comprehend what we have, a force of power to be used for our benefit, we will not so easily allow joy to be taken up or away from us. Loud opposing voices will not alarm us to surrender it, for our minds will not be in suspense, wondering if it is ours to keep. We, in joy, will keep a strong hold of it as a very valuable treasure, because we will have the ability to protect it from loss.

The last phrase is "your joy will be complete". We must be assured that God wants us to be fully complete in everything He gives us, including joy, therefore, we must never settle for anything less. The disciples never thought joy had to come through the death and resurrection of Jesus. We have a better advantage, because we do not have to wait for it, for joy is already a completed fact. We just need to receive joy by faith and live in it, strengthened.

Colossians 2:5 states: "For though I am absent from you in body, I am present with you in spirit and delight to see how orderly you are and how firm your faith in Christ is". NIV. The word "delight" produces from within a calmly happy and well-off attitude. We, in turn, prosper, gain health and vitality in all aspects of our lives. Paul was writing about his joy or delight of the Colossians' actions in their lives of faith.

The word "see" is defined (S): "to look at, which denotes voluntary observation". When our joy is in action, it will be seen by all who choose to look with voluntary observation. Any and all observation takes time and effort, therefore it must captivate their interest. God's kind of joy strengthens us where we can victoriously overcome the problem or adversity and it cannot be denied for it will be obvious. Paul took notice, for the results were obvious, what the Colossians were doing with their faith.

The first obvious sign for joy is "orderly"' defined (S): "regular arrangement, that is (in time) fixed succession (of rank or character),

Joy: the first step on the foundation of love

official dignity", and (D): *"a condition in which each thing is properly disposed with reference to other things and to its purpose".* **An alternate version: "standing shoulder to shoulder in such orderly array". AMP.**

The functions of the fruit of the Spirit are never chaotic, but orderly. Joy has a regular arrangement to its actions, therefore the fixed successions over time marks out the rank or character of the person, and by this we know whether we are operating in joy or not. We have official Godly joy or dignity and it keeps us in control over the problem or adversity. This inner strength, that comes from joy, maintains our cause, just like Paul took notice in the Colossians.

The second obvious sign for joy is "firm" defined (S): "something established, that is (abstract) confirmation (stability)", and (D): *"fixed in direction; literally means fixed in place, but used figuratively to indicate undeviating constancy or resolution".* **An alternate version: "firmness, solid front". AMP.**

Joy is orderly, steady and established, therefore stable. When we operate in joy, we become undeviatingly constant against the problem or adversity. The longer we stand in joy, the stronger we become, in contrast, the longer we stand in the flesh, the weaker we will become. The longer we stand in joy, we will develop within our spirit more strength, and will less likely give it up. Paul saw this, that the Colossians' joy was orderly and steadfast, holding their faith strong, thereby pleasing God.

II Corinthians 8:2; "Out of the most severe trial, their overflowing joy and their extreme poverty welled up in rich generosity". NIV.

The word "most" is defined (S): "much (in any respect); many", the word "trial" is defined (S): "test "abstract or concrete); by implication, trustiness", and the word "severe" is defined (S): "pressure (literally or figuratively)".

The phrase "Out of the most severe trial" was stated for the Corinthians' continual persecutions for their faith, thereby making them low class citizens, and losing their means of earning sufficient money. When we put the definitions together, we get: *"much (in any respect) tests, trustiness or (proof of) the pressure".* **An alternate version: "ordeal of severe tribulation". AMP.**

These persecutions were not superficial, but ran deep within their livelihood, where they lost their jobs, homes and status for their faith. The Corinthians knew the consequences for their actions, yet wholeheartedly kept on living in faith, knowing that at the end, they would receive more then they lost. How about us, when someone makes fun of us or mocks us for our faith, should we just give into them?

The next phrase "their overflowing joy", the word "overflowing" is defined (S): "surplusage, that is superabundance", and (D): "an extremely plentiful or over sufficient quantity or supply".

The Corinthians had overflowing joy, in other words, a surplus or extremely plentiful/over-sufficient quantity of joy. They didn't allow their afflictions to tear down their joy, but decided to build up within themselves this joy, until nothing could stop them.

The water that comes out from the fountain spout cannot easily be stopped when it is flowing. The faster and harder the flow of water, the harder it is to stop. Therefore, the more we build up our joy, the more it will strengthen or fortify us, getting us superabundantly charged where no affliction can stop it. This, the Corinthians did, when their affliction came in the form of poverty.

The next phrase "their extreme poverty", the words "extreme" is defined (S): "deep, in other words, profundity (to reach down deeply), that is (by implication) extent; (figuratively) mystery", and "poverty" (S): "beggary, that is indigence (literally or figuratively)', and (D): "lacking food, clothing or other necessities of life because of poverty; needy, impoverished".

Paul wrote that the Corinthians were-very destitute, so to speak they were not on the bottom of the barrel, but underneath. This affliction did not stop them, because their joy was so over-surplussed, that they anticipated and expected to be able to give abundantly.

Many of us Christians today, when we get financially strapped, hoard our money. The more we hoard, the less we actually have, since it is taken out of circulation, where no one can use it, including the person hoarding it. Luke 8:16-18: states that everything has a purpose and it must be used. **Luke 8:18b: states "whoever does not have (whenever we hoard, it is as if we do not have it, since we cannot use ourselves), even what he thinks he has will be taken from him". NIV.**

We, Christians, must possess a joyful attitude, before we will ever overcome our afflictions victoriously. The Corinthians gave in joy, knowing that from joy comes strength, and gave them the ability to give without fear, because they were fortified. This looks mysterious to the world that we would give, as the Corinthians did then, when we are short of supply.

The last phrase "welled up in rich generosity", the word "welled up" is defined (S): "to super-abound (in quantity and quality), be in excess, be superfluous (being more than is sufficient or required)", and "rich" is defined (S): "wealth (as fullness), that is (literally) money, possessions, or (figuratively) abundance, richness, (specifically) valuable bestowment", and "generosity" is defined (S): "singleness, that is (subjectively) sincerely (without dissimulation (cover-up) or self-seek-

Joy: the first step on the foundation of love

ing), or (objectively) generosity (copious bestowal)", and (D): "the quality or condition of being liberal in giving".

The Corinthians showed what character they had, when they decided to overflow in joy which strengthened them, in spite of the affliction/persecutions against them. They desired, in spite of their extreme poverty, to overflow/well-up in giving richly, both in quantity and quality, and were superfluous in doing more than is sufficient or required of them. **II Corinthians 8:12: "For if the willingness is there, the gift is acceptable according to what one has, not according to what he does not have"**. NIV, God looks at what is in our heart, and if our heart is right, then it is supported by joy which strengthens us to give willingly.

The Corinthians gave what was of valuable bestowment, that is wealth in fulness, and also gave their best of what they had in possessions. The Corinthians gave from their hearts and put value to their giving, thereby God honored it. Our giving must be the quality according to what is in our heart, backed-up with the quantity according to what we have.

The Corinthians' giving was generous because it was with singleness or sincerity. They did not dissimulate (cover-up) or self-seek to satisfy their personal needs, but sought how to meet the needs of others. They were so willing to give that they begged to give. (see II Corinthians 8:3-6).

Today, we Christians must come to realize the power in giving, where all the churches would flourish and be able to proclaim the Gospel properly funded. Pastors wouldn't resort to begging, but have the surplus to meet the needs of the poor making it easier for them to see the value of salvation. The affluent will only respond to successful organizations, where their wealth is protected, therefore the church must project this image to attract them and also present them the Gospel. Only joy can strengthen our hearts to give, and to stand strong in a fortified place and a defense in proclaiming the Gospel.

Let's summarize on our study of joy. Joy is not a fleeting emotional feeling, but strength that comes by a fortified place and a defense, and gives us the ability to celebrate. We are to expect joy, given by Jesus, to take up full time residence in us, and fill us to overflowing. True joy cannot be taken from us, and is orderly and steadfast, where we can always rely on it. We must continually build-up our joy until overflowing to stand against any affliction. Joy operates properly on the foundation of love, the first function of the fruit of the Spirit, which enriches us with strength.

5

Peace: the second step on the foundation of love

The preceding chapters covered love and joy. Love was found to be the willingly giving of oneself to another to meet their real need, and is never self-serving. Love is the first fundamental attribute of God, therefore it must be the foundation on which everything is supported. Joy is not a fleeting emotional feeling, but the very strength of God Himself, which fortifies us and places us in a defense. The joy placed within us must be built-up to become strong and not have it stolen from us. Joy is orderly and steadfast, and we can totally rely on it.

The third function of the fruit of the Spirit is peace. The world has its own idea of peace, and is always trying to attain it, yet it never does. Chaos and disorder is in the heart of man, and man doesn't have the ability to produce peace on their own, without God, *The dictionary defines peace: "the normal, non-warring condition of a nation; a state of mutual harmony between people; freedom of the mind from annoyance, distraction, anxiety, and an obsession; cessation of or freedom of any strife or dissension".* We notice that these define the superficial or outward appearance of peace. It never deals with the real root of the problem, therefore the peace it offers can never stay permanently.

God, however, provides for us peace that far exceeds anything that we can discover on our own. God desires for us to have this kind of peace, which is permanent, and is there always for our disposal.

"Peace" is defined (S): "peace (literally or figuratively); by implication prosperity; (to join)", where "to join" is defined (D): "to enlist in one of the armed forces; to meet or engage in battle or conflict" The UN troops are sent out, even to fight back the opposition to keep peace. We, looking at it this way, can better understand the purpose God had in mind for peace. God has given us the ability to fight back the enemy, Satan, from stealing our peace, and to maintain our rightful position God has given us.

Peace: the second step on the foundation of love

The first Scripture is found in John 14:27a: "Peace I leave with you; my peace I give you, I do not give to you as the world gives". NIV. *The word "leave" is defined (S): "leave; to send forth", and (D): "to give for use after one's death or departure".* This describes a type of will or covenant promise, and can be received only after the person dies or departs the scene. Jesus promised to leave peace to us after His resurrection, which is now in effect.

The word "give" is defined (S): "to give (used in a very wide application)", and (D): "to present voluntarily and without expecting compensation; to furnish, provide or proffer (to place before for acceptance); to pledge, offer as a pledge or execute and deliver".

Jesus gave us the peace, done voluntarily on His part, without expecting compensation from us, but placed it before us for acceptance on our part. We cannot blame God for not having peace or beg God to give it to us, for He has already offered it to us as a pledge, executed it for us and delivered it to us. We need to take this gift of peace and let it produce fruit in our lives.

If someone gave us a gift, but we refused to accept it, it would be considered a rude act on our part. How much ruder would it be, if we decided not to accept the gift of peace from God, since all the gifts from God are for our benefit? **James 1:17 states: "Every good and perfect gift is from above, coming down from the Father of the heavenly lights, who does not change like shifting shadows". NIV.**

The second Scripture is found in John 14:27b: "Do not let your hearts be troubled and do not be afraid". NIV. *The word "troubled" is defined (S): "to stir or agitate (roil water= to render turbid by stirring up sediment)".*

There are people who constantly cause trouble, because within themselves, they lack peace and cannot stand others who have peace in their lives. They try to stir up the past, in other words, to roil up the situation, striving to break down the peace.

Peace has been given as a gift in the fruit of the Spirit, therefore we are to stand continually, enjoying the victory, not become subject to the stirring up of the past. We, in peace, are acting properly before God and man, holding our ground, which rightfully belongs to us. **Two Scriptures that support this are: Philippians 3:13b-14: "But one thing I do: Forgetting what is behind and straining toward what is ahead, I press on toward the goal to win the prize for which God has called me heavenward in Christ Jesus", and Luke 9:62: "Jesus replied, No one who puts his hand to the plow and looks back is fit for service in the Kingdom of God". NIV.**

The second word "afraid" is defined (S) "to be timid", and (D): "timid; lacking in self-assurance, courage or fearlessness; easily alarmed; timorous; shy".

There is nothing we need to be afraid of, when operating in the peace from God. We have the required ability, from peace, to push back the enemy. The UN peacekeeping troops, likewise with authority, pushes back the one side apart from the other. This peace, from God, not only pushes back the enemy, but gives us the dominion and authority to take back what the enemy stole from us.

We cannot afford the luxury of lacking self-assurance and courage, and be easily alarmed. The enemy, Satan, continually tries to put up a front against us, even though we have peace on our side. Therefore, we are the ones to prosper and to be victorious over any attacks against us. **II Timothy 1:7 states: "For God did not give us a spirit of timidity, but a spirit of power, of love and of self-discipline". NIV.** God does not give timidity, therefore we do not have to receive it, for it is from the enemy, Satan, who is ever trying to tear us down.

Peace from God affects our heart, therefore we must not allow anything contrary to render it ineffective. Peace has the inherent property to protect us from trouble and fear. **The Amplified version states very appropriately: "(stop allowing yourselves to be agitated and disturbed; and do not permit to be fearful and intimidated and cowardly and unsettled)".** We must stop allowing or permitting the situation or adversity to steal our peace, since we have dominion over it by peace.

Jesus was promising peace to the disciples, yet they did not comprehend how this peace would be theirs. Jesus fulfilled this promise after His death and resurrection. When Jesus appeared to them they were frightened because they didn't receive the offered fulfilled promise of peace as of yet. The rest is history as how the disciples grew in peace, after they decided to receive it. This peace that was offered to the disciples is offered to us in the same way, for God is not partial to anyone, therefore it is in operation today.

The next Scripture is found in John 16:33a: "I have told you these things, so that in me you may have peace". NIV. *The word "may have" is defined (S): "to hold (used in very various applications such as possession, ability, contiguity, relation or condition)".*

Jesus proclaimed, that in Him, we have peace, therefore we must come to Him to obtain it. It is up to us to hold onto peace, once we obtain it, and take possession of the same, for in possessing this peace, we acquire its ability. Peace becomes contiguious (surrounds us), when we hold onto it and develop a relationship with it. We get into position, over a period of time, to determine the condition of peace we choose to live in.

The second part is found in John 16:33b: "In this world you will have trouble. But take heart! I have overcome the world".

NIV. *The word "world" is defined (S): "world as an orderly arrangement, that is decoration; by implication the world".* It is the Greek word "kosmos", in other words, the atmosphere around us (which is orderly and decorated for us), that affect our lives. *The word "trouble" is defined (S): "pressure (literally or figuratively)", and (D): "grievous trouble; severe trial or suffering; an affliction",* **and an alternate version: "tribulation and trials and distress and frustrations". AMP.** Trouble without recourse, would make us hopeless, but Jesus continued His discourse and told us to "take heart". **An alternate version states: "(take courage; be confident, certain, undaunted)". AMP.**

The words "have overcome" is defined (S): "to subdue (literally or figuratively); conquest (abstract), that is (figuratively) the means of success", and (Y): "to gain the victory", and (D): "to get the better of in a struggle or conflict; conquer; defeat".

Jesus proclaimed His victory for us, where we have peace from Him, and can totally rely on Him for our ability to push back the enemy. The sole purpose of Jesus was to subdue the works of the enemy on mankind, through His death and resurrection, where He made the conquest and won, therefore He now has the means of success for us.

Satan still has rule in this world, and those who choose not to believe in Jesus, are still under his subjection whether they agree or not. We believers no longer need to be under his control and subjection, since Jesus already provided the means of success over Satan. We must apprehend this gift of peace and become prosperous in what we do, totally above the dictates of Satan. **An alternate version states: "I have deprived it of power to harm you and have conquered it for you". AMP.**

The word "world" has a dual meaning, the worldly system we operate in, and our fleshly bodies trained by this worldly system, even though we are now positionally above it through peace. We can overcome the ungodly desires of the flesh and bring it under control with this peace. We must attack two fronts that are against us and develop success because of this peace.

God's gifts are always for our total benefit, therefore we, believers, have total rights to apply it in our lives. We don't need to hunt for it or beg God for it, since it is implanted into us the moment we ask Jesus into our hearts, as He said, "...that in me you may have peace".

The next Scripture is Philippians 4:7: "And the peace of God, which transcends all understanding, will guard your hearts and your minds in Christ Jesus". NIV. An alternate version amplifies peace; "(shall be yours that tranquil state of the soul assured of its salvation through Christ, and so fearing nothing from God and being content with its earthly lot of whatever sort it is, that peace)". AMP.

This peace gives us the tranquil assurance, no fear from God and earthly contentment, and we are always better off, since it also means prosperity and success.

The word "transcends" is defined (S): "to hold oneself above, that is (figuratively) to excel", and (D): "to go beyond (a point, degree, stage, etc.)"; transcend; exceed; surpass". The word "understanding" is defined (S): "the intellect, that is mind (divine or human; in thought, feeling or will); by implication meaning", and (D): "knowledge of or familiarity with a familiar thing; skill in dealing with or handling something".

God's peace does not come from this limited natural world, but from the spiritual world and holds itself above this world, therefore it always excels. This peace will bring us beyond any point, degree, stage, etc. and hold us above this world's limitations.

When we use our natural understanding, we automatically limit and hinder ourselves from what God had planned for us. Our natural understanding is always based on what we already know and are familiar with, therefore we use these skills to deal with the afflictions, hoping to solve them. We get dismayed, when the afflictions do not go away but continue to haunt us to the point where we give into it as a hopeless cause.

God never desires for us to give into any affliction, therefore he gave us peace, which causes us to hold above it, that is, to excel over it as victors. His peace far transcends or surpasses anything we can think of, because our natural understanding is limited by our unregenerated, worldly trained minds. Our minds include thought, feeling, and will, and if not trained according to God's word, it is hopeless to ever come to fully understand.

Romans 12:2 states: "Do not conform any longer to the pattern of this world, but be transformed by the renewing of your mind. Then you will be able to test and approve what God's will is—his good, pleasing and perfect will". NIV. This Scripture states that our minds must be retrained and renewed with God's word to think like He does. Then we will more readily accept God's peace in our lives, thereby acting accordingly to receive the benefits.

The word "guard" is defined (S): "to be a watcher in advance, that is to mount a guard as a sentinel (post spies at gates); to guard; to protect".

We must ascertain that peace has reliance on a fortification or a defense, which is joy, and God's peace is like a watcher in advance. This peace within us, will alert in place, time or state, which only one person can do all that—Jesus, and it is also the instrumentality medially (centrally) and constructively on how peace comes to us —in the person of Jesus. Peace, therefore, can only come by the way of Jesus, either way we look at it, when we decide to receive Jesus as our Lord and Savior.

Peace: the second step on the foundation of love

The final Scripture on peace is Colossians 3:15: "Let the peace of Christ rule in your hearts, since as members of one body you were called to peace. And be thankful". NIV. *The word "rule" is defined (S): "to arbitrate, that is (generally) to govern (figuratively) prevail".* The word "arbitrate" is defined (D): *"to submit to the hearing and determining of a dispute between parties by a person or persons chosen or agreed to by them"*, and *"prevail"* is defined (D): *"to appear or occur as the more important or frequent feature or element...to be or proved superior in strength, power or influence... to use persuasion or inducement successfully".*

Jesus had the hearing and determination of the dispute between God and Satan, and He has won the case. We will always have disputes in this world, for it can not be avoided, but we do not have to be subject to them without any recourse. When we decide to accept and receive the salvation from God, we are set free from Satan to God. We are now in peace when we believe, because we have the same determination as Jesus has, and the ruling is, we have peace from God.

This peace God has given us must have our participation, and have our full submission to God's plan, in order for peace to be effective in our lives. We can possess this peace, and yet receive none of the benefits from it, therefore we must allow peace to have the more important, frequent feature or element in our lives, rather than the affliction. This peace must be or proven superior in strength, power or influence over any affliction we will ever face. We must allow or permit this peace to persuade or induce us to successfully, on our behalf, to jettison and put us over the affliction, thereby being and living victoriously. An alternate version develops this in an appropriate way, in what God was wanting us to understand: **"(act as an umpire continually) ...(deciding and settling with finality all questions that arise in our minds, in that peaceful state)". AMP.**

We will explore the second portion of this Scripture, with the first word "called" defined (S): *"to call (properly loud)"*. and (D): *"to cry out in a loud voice...to announce authoritatively; proclaim; order...to summon by or as if by divine command"*

This peace from God is a loud call or command, therefore we must rally behind this call, unifying ourselves together into one body. This call of peace was sent out as an authoritative announcement or proclamation for us believers, setting us together to fight against the common enemy, Satan. We must be unified by the means of this peace, to support one another, shoulder to shoulder against any affliction, therefore standing victoriously.

The second word is "thankful" defined (S): *"well-favored, that is (by implication) grateful"*, and (D): *"feeling or expressing gratitude or acknowledgement to"*. *The Greek word is "Eucharistos", where we derive the word Eucharist or Communion, and is defined (D): "the consecrated elements of the Holy Communion...the giving of thanks".*

We must keep this peace well-favored, whereby we will totally submit to and fully rely on the benefits derived. If we foolishly neglect to be thankful, we must not think we can operate in this peace. Any and all things from God must be fully appreciated, in order for God to release the benefits attributed to the gift. **An alternate version states: "(appreciative, giving praise to God always)". AMP.**

Let us summarize our coverage on "peace", which is by no means exhausting this subject. We discovered many interesting elements within God's idea of peace, therefore we no longer have to settle for the world's idea of peace, which has no real lasting substance.

Jesus proclaimed, that God's peace was left or sent forth for us, and was given voluntarily, therefore we must decide to accept and receive it for ourselves. We, with this peace, do not need to fear any affliction.

When we obtain this peace, we must hold onto it to prevent loss to the enemy. We know afflictions are in this world, yet we do not need to submit, because Jesus already overcame the source of it, Satan.

God's peace will keep, guard or protect us in our hearts and minds. Peace gives us a tranquil assurance, and comes from the unlimited spiritual world. If we totally rely on this peace, it will not be hindered by our limited natural understanding, but it will help us obtain prosperity and success in all that we do.

God commands us to let peace rule (arbitrate) in our hearts, because Jesus already settled the dispute between God and Satan. We, by our actions, within this peace, must fully participate in it in order to receive the benefits, by making it the most important influence in our lives and be persuaded of its success.

This peace was loudly proclaimed with authority, therefore we must rally behind it together, shoulder to shoulder, and we must be thankful for our continual victory over our afflictions.

These three functions of the fruit of the Spirit, love, joy and peace, has its primary function or purpose upon our spirit man. These cause us to be like God, like in love we become true givers, in joy we become strengthened, and in peace we become a fighter against the enemy.

6

Longsuffering: the third step on the foundation of love

We now enter the next phase of the fruit of the Spirit; longsuffering, gentleness, and goodness. These three have its primary function upon our soul; our will, emotion, and intellect/mind.

The fourth function of the fruit of the Spirit is *longsuffering, which is defined (S): "longanimity (patient endurance of hardships or injuries), that is (objectively) forbearance, or (subjectively) patient", and (D): "enduring injury or provocation long and patiently".* **An alternate version; "(an even temper, forbearance)". AMP.** This word is a two part compound in Greek. The first is "long in time", and the second is "passion (as if breathing hard)". When put together, we get "long in time passion", in other words, "we breathe hard while waiting patiently", something like we do in counting to ten before we react. We, by this, prevent ourselves from doing something foolish.

Several Scriptures describe God as longsuffering:

Exodus 34:6: "And he passed in front of Moses, proclaiming, 'The Lord, the Lord, the compassionate and gracious God, SLOW TO ANGER, abounding in love and faithfulness,". NIV.

Numbers 14:18: "The Lord is SLOW TO ANGER, abounding in love and forgiving sin and rebellion.". NIV.

Psalms 86:15: "But you, O Lord, are a compassionate and gracious God, SLOW TO ANGER, abounding in love and faithfulness". NIV.

Jeremiah 15:15: "You understand, O Lord; remember me and care for me. Avenge me on my persecutors. You

are LONG-SUFFERING—do not take me away; think of how I suffer reproach for your sake". NIV.

The concluding Scripture is **Psalms 103:8: "The Lord is compassionate and gracious, SLOW TO ANGER, abounding in love". NIV.** *"Slow" is defined (S): "long; to be (causative mode), long (figuratively or literally)", while "anger" (S): "(from the rapid breathing in passion); ire (anger, wrath)".*

"Slow to anger" is therefore defined "to be long towards anger or wrath". God does not flare up instantly, but chooses to be long in time before He becomes angry. Since this is the characteristic of God, and He placed longsuffering within our hearts when we became believers, therefore we must exhibit this same characteristic.

Our next Scripture is found in **Nehemiah 9:17: "They refused to listen and failed to remember the miracles you performed among them. They became stiff-necked and in their rebellion appointed a leader in order to return to their slavery. But you are a forgiving God, gracious and compassionate, SLOW TO ANGER and abounding in love. Therefore you did not desert them,". NIV.**

There was constant rebellion from the Israeli, from the Egyptian exodus to the Babylonian captivity, yet God was always ready to forgive (slow to anger). God never lashed out His anger because of Israel's rebellion, even after repeated warnings. He only released His anger, when the Israeli came to the point of total rebellion against God and showed no sign whatsoever of turning back.

We notice here how God handled the rebellious and difficult Israelis, and we must show the same concerted effort in being slow to anger. People, for the most part, are rebellious in nature, therefore when two or more people come together, there will be resistance developed against new ideas and ways presented. We can decide to become angry instantly or to wait, preferably for a long time, and save ourselves useless anger because the differences can be smoothed out without confrontation. When something is obviously wrong, we must correct it quickly, yet in longsuffering even if anger is needed.

Psalms 145:8 states that God is "slow to anger". This was placed within the setting of praise and proclamation to the awesome works and great deeds of God. God demonstrates His actions of longsuffering, where man can see and follow. Longsuffering or slow to anger is considered an awesome work and a great deed, therefore we must decide to act accordingly and manifest these for others to see and follow.

Proverbs 14:29 states "A patient man has great understanding, but a quick-tempered man displays folly". NIV. *"Great*

Longsuffering: the third step on the foundation of love

understanding" is defined (S): *"intelligence; by implication an argument; by extension caprice"*, and (D): *"to be thoroughly familiar with; apprehend clearly the character, nature or subtleties of"*. *"Argument"* is defined (D): *"a process of reasoning; an address or composition intended to convince or persuade"*, and *"caprice"* (D): *"a sudden, unpredictable change, as one's mind"*.

Longsuffering or slow to anger creates within us a great understanding, where we can apprehend clearly or see through unhindered the character, nature or subtleties of the person or thing. The argument, therefore, can be settled reasonably, where we can address the situation with the intent to convince or persuade the person involved to think about our rationale, because positive arguments reason , while the negative don't. The attitude of longsuffering gives us the ability to be sudden and have an unpredictable change in our minds, in other words to think quickly, therefore possibly resolving the problems.

"Quick-tempered" is defined (S): *"short (whether in size, number, life, strength or anger/temper)"*. *"Displays"* is defined (S): *"to be high actively; to rise or raise"*, and (D): *"to elevate in rank, honor, power, character, quality etc."*. *"Folly"* is defined (S): *"silliness"*, and (D): *"state or quality of being foolish; lack of understanding or sense"*.

When we decide not to do longsuffering, it adds to the existing problem. A quick-tempered person cannot operate in love, therefore looking within for self-satisfaction, displaying or raising his estimation of himself, and exposing folly or silliness. When we elevate ourselves, in quality or state without understanding or sense over the problems, we take it farther away from the solution.

Proverbs 15:18 states "A hot-tempered man stirs up dissension, but a patient man calms a quarrel". NIV. *"Calms"* is defined (S): *"to repose (the state of being at rest); calm; (to settle down)"*, and (D): *"to bring to a point or state of peace, quiet, ease or contentment; to yield or concede to the belligerent demands of a person in an effort to overcome the distrust or hostility; win over"*. *"'Quarrel,'* is defined (S): *"a contest (personal or legal)"'*, and (D): *"a vigorous or bitter conflict, discord or antagonism"*.

This Scripture indicates to us that longsuffering or slow to anger seeks to calm down the situation by looking for a way to win over the person by showing concerted effort to overcome distrust or hostility. Longsuffering is never in a contest or bitter conflict, discord or antagonism against any person. When we operate in longsuffering or slow to anger, we have the ability to appease, pacify or calm strife, contentions or quarrels.

Proverbs 16:32 states: "Better a patient man than a warrior, a man who controls his temper than one who takes a city".

NIV. *"Better" is defined (S): "better, as good used in the widest sense", and (D): "morally superior; more virtuous".* *"Warrior" is defined (S): "powerful; by implication warrior, tyrant", and (D): "having, characterized by or showing might or power like a person who shows great vigor, courage or aggressiveness".*

The Bible states here, in a morally superior and more virtuous way, that it is good when we exert qualities of longsuffering or patience, therefore manifesting a better way. We will become more convincing of our way of thinking when acting in patience, because persuasion comes through presenting the ideas that are proven to work than pushing non-proven ideas. When in longsuffering or patience, we will not be hasty because if the proven idea works now, it will work later.

An interesting Scripture is **James 1:19: "My dear brothers, take note of this: Everyone should be quick to listen, slow to speak, and slow to become angry,".** NIV. God states that we are to be quick to listen, but slow to speak. When we decide to be quick to listen, we become teachable, therefore when we speak we will not say foolishness and exhibit anger. Isn't it interesting that God knows what we need to control: our tongue and anger?

II Peter 3:15a states "Bear in mind that our Lord's patience means salvation,". NIV. *"Bear in mind" is defined (S): "to lead, that is command (with official authority); figuratively to deem, that is consider".*

We must lead or command our minds with official authority from God, and deem or consider what God says far more important than what we feel, since the longsuffering of our Lord will produce in our lives. We must set our hearts and minds on what God says and work patiently or with longsuffering to obtain the benefits.

"Salvation" is defined (S): "rescue or safety (physical or moral)", and (Y): "soundness", and (D): "the act of saving or protecting from harm, risk, loss, destruction, etc.".

We must pay close attention, in order to see that salvation is more than a ticket to heaven. Salvation is a rescue and a safety both moral (spirit and soul), and physical (body, social and finances), therefore God wants soundness for our whole man, now in this life, as well as in the life to come. Consequently, when we operate in longsuffering, we derive beyond our normal self-defeating attitudes and ideas of ourselves, and look to what God strongly desires us to have. Longsuffering positions us to receive the fullness of this given salvation. All we need to do is believe it, and then to act on it, to receive the rightful benefits for our corresponding actions. **An alternate version concurs: "and consider that the longsuffering of the Lord (His slowness in avenging**

Longsuffering: the third step on the foundation of love

wrongs and judging the world) is salvation (that which is conducive to the soul's safety)...". AMP.

II Timothy 4:2 states "Preach the Word; be prepared in season and out of season; correct, rebuke and encourage—with great patience and careful instruction". NIV. Let's look at three words: 1-correct, 2-rebuke, 3-encourage. "Correct" is defined (S): "to confute (to prove false), admonish", and (D): "to address words of disapproval of". "Rebuke" is defined (S): "to tax upon, that is censure (strong expression of disapproval), or admonish", and (D): "to express sharp, stern disapproval of". "Encourage" is defined (S): "to call near, that is invite, invoke", and (D): "to urge, advise or caution earnestly".

We have a strong command, therefore must be prepared to carry it out at all times. We, with great patience and careful instruction, must remain faithful to the truth of the Word of God. This was the setting where Paul was instructing Timothy to be prepared in and out of season. What was Timothy to be prepared for?

Timothy had to correct or prove false some for moving off sound doctrine, in other words, he had to address their actions with words of disapproval. Others who were moved far off sound doctrine, he had to censure or express strong disapproval, in other words, he expressed sharp, stern disapproval of their motives. The third group who had not left sound doctrine, he encouraged and called near as an invitation or earnest desire in supplication, in other words, he urged, advised and cautioned earnestly to stay with sound doctrine at all costs.

This command can only be fulfilled by operating in longsuffering. If we lash out at those, who are in error or false doctrine, they will not be won over to the truth, because their nature is to hang onto what they already believe. We must persuade them by being patient, proving to them the errors of their ways, thereby being able to correct, rebuke and encourage them on their way back by great patience and careful instruction.

Colossians 3:12 states, "Therefore, as God's chosen people, holy and dearly loved, clothe yourselves with compassion, kindness, humility, gentleness and patience". NIV "Clothe yourselves" is defined (S): "(in a sense sinking into a garment); to invest with clothing (literally or figuratively)", and (D): "to clothe oneself; to assume, adopt".

Where are clothes put on? Naturally on the outside of our body, where everyone can see what we are wearing. God also desires for us to clothe ourselves with the attribute of longsuffering, where it can be seen by others. Longsuffering, as well as the other functions of the Fruit of the Spirit, must be seen by other, so that they will desire it for themselves.

The final Scripture is **Ephesians 4:1-3 which states, "As a prisoner for the Lord, then, I urge you to live a life worthy of the** calling you have received. Be completely humble and gentle; be patient, bearing with one another in love. Make every effort to keep the unity of the Spirit through the bond of peace". NIV. Six words will be described: 1-bearing with one another, 2-make every effort, 3-keep, 4-unity, 5-bond , 6-peace. "Bearing with one another" is defined (S): "to hold oneself up against, that is (figuratively) put up with", and (D): "to be patient or self-controlled when subject to annoyances or provocations". "Make every effort" is defined (S): "to use speed, that is to make effort, be prompt or earnest", and (D): "to exert oneself to do or effect something; make an effort; strive". "Keep" is defined (S): "to guard (from loss or injury, properly by keeping the eye upon", and (D): "to maintain (same position), especially in accordance with specific requirements". "Unity" is defined (S): "oneness, that is (figuratively) unanimity", and (D): "the state of being one; oneness; undivided opinion". "Bond" is defined (S): "a joint tie, that is ligament, (figuratively) uniting principle, control", and (D): "something that binds a person to a certain line of behavior". "Peace" is defined as to join, like into a military situation, thereby fighting back the enemy and keeping peace resulting in prosperity.

Longsuffering effects a lot of situations when used properly. Longsuffering aides us to bear with others and be self-controlled when dealing with others, and brings about every effort where we keep from loss and maintain with specific requirements. It develops unity or oneness, in other words, undivided opinions, whereby we, in a certain line of behavior, have a joint tie or bond leading to peace.

An alternate version states: "I therefore, the prisoner for the Lord, appeal to and beg you to walk (lead a life) worthy of the (divine) calling to which you have been called (with behavior that is a credit to the summons to God's service, (living as becomes you) with complete lowliness of mind (humility) and meekness (unselfishness, gentleness, mildness), with patience, bearing with one anther and making allowances because you love one another. Be eager and strive earnestly to guard and keep the harmony and oneness of (and produced by) the Spirit in the binding power of peace". AMP.

Let us summarize on this subject of longsuffering. Longsuffering is patient endurance of hardships or injuries, like when we count to ten before we act, which prevents foolish actions. It chooses not to flare up in anger but waits long before taking actions, which is a characteristic of God, and we must exhibit this quality. It is considered a great act within a setting of praise and testimony, and is to be seen and followed by others.

Longsuffering moreover has great understanding, and we acquire intelligence where we can familiarize ourselves and see clearer the nature,

Longsuffering: the third step on the foundation of love

character or subtleties of the person or thing. When we operate this way, we then can reason with the intent to persuade or convince.

Longsuffering looks for ways to appease or calm down the situation at hand. It never seeks to be in a contest, bitter conflict, discord or antagonism against anyone, and also yields to the belligerent demands in an effort to break down distrust or hostility.

Longsuffering is never hasty or pushy, demanding our own way. It is good, morally superior and more virtuous, when we manifest longsuffering, being more convincing by proven ways than nonproven ways.

Longsuffering takes in account, leading and commanding our minds with official authority from God, placing us in position to receive, where we can acquire the full benefits of our salvation. Salvation is not just a ticket to heaven, but it is a rescue and safety for the whole man: spirit, soul, body, social and finances.

Longsuffering does not lash out at the faults and errors of others, therefore we can correct, rebuke and encourage them. They can then see their error and we can lead them back to sound doctrine or careful instruction.

God desires us to wear, like clothing, longsuffering, and this is done so that others can see it in action and eventually desire it for themselves.

We, in longsuffering, must rely on the previous functions of the fruit of the Spirit, and each function is another step on the foundation of love. Longsuffering originates from the spirit and it operate through the soul, giving us the ability to think straight without lashing out emotionally.

7

Gentleness: the fourth step on the foundation of love

We found in the previous chapter, that longsuffering was patient endurance, a great act, has great understanding, looks to calm down, not hasty or pushy, led by God's official authority, able to correct, rebuke and encourage without faultfinding, and it is worn, like clothes, for everyone to see. God placed longsuffering within us, where we can manifest this as God had planned it to work. This is the first function of the fruit of the Spirit, where we can control our minds.

The fifth function of the fruit of the Spirit is called *"gentleness"*, and is defined (S): *"usefulness, that is moral excellence (in character or demeanor)"*, and (Y): *"kindness, usefulness"*, and (D): *"disposition or behavior, and often suggests a deliberate or voluntary kindness or forbearance in dealing with others; a sympathetic attitude towards others and a willingness to do good or give pleasure; a deep seated characteristic shown either habitually or on occasion by considerate behavior"*. An alternate reference: *"a disposition to be gentle, soft-spoken, kind, even-tempered, cultured and refined in character or conduct"*. DAKES.

Gentleness is not being weak or caving into the situation, but is a strong function of usefulness. Gentleness displays a moral excellence in character or demeanor, and works when we set ourselves focused continually towards ministering to others for their good. Gentleness will, then, be useful for others and ourselves to benefit from.

An example, in Daniel 3:16-18, where the three Hebrew boys were facing a real predicament. They were going to be thrown in the fiery furnace, yet they remained faithful to God in gentleness, which manifested their moral excellence or demeanor. They refused to fight or struggle against the king to escape, but believed God would deliver them no mat-

Gentleness: the fourth step on the foundation of love 41

ter what the king would do. Needless to say, God delivered them and in turn the king, also, became a believer.

I Peter 3:1-12 writes on how we ought to conduct ourselves with each other. It describes how a wife should conduct herself with her husband, by not being pushy or flashy, but allowing her gentle and quiet spirit to operate, manifesting God's love, where he would be won over. It, also, describes how a husband must treat his wife with respect. It, finally, describes how we must treat each other by being compassionate and not repaying evil and insult back to evil done to us. Gentleness always manifests moral excellence in character or demeanor, which produces love, sympathy, harmony, compassion and humility.

II Timothy 2:24-26 states; "And the Lord's servant must not quarrel; instead, he must be kind to everyone, able to teach, not resentful. Those who oppose him he must gently instruct, in the hope that God will grant them repentance leading them to the knowledge of the truth, and that they will come to their senses and escape from the trap of the devil, who has taken them captive to do his will". NIV. *"Quarrel" is defined (S): "to war, that is (figuratively) to quarrel", and (D): "to contend in opposition, battle or any conflict; compete; to struggle vigorously as in opposition or resistance". Another reference: "to fight, contend in battle, quarrel, wrangle and dispute". DAKES.*

We, as the servants of the Lord, must not quarrel, or allow the war, quarrel or dispute to enter into our lives. We are not in competition against each other, where we struggle vigorously as in opposition or resistance, but must be drawn to each other. How do we create an atmosphere, where we are brought together and not separated by quarrels?

The second word "kind" is defined (S): "affable, that is mild or kind", and (D): "pleasantly easy to talk to; showing warmth and friendliness; civil". **An alternate version states: "be kindly to everyone and mild-tempered (preserving the bond of peace)". AMP.**

Gentleness is not a mark of weakness, but usefulness and having a moral excellence in character or demeanor, therefore it is required of us to be gentle to others. When in gentleness, we manifest affability, in other words, pleasantly easy to talk to and showing warmth and friendliness. Unwanted barriers can come down, where we are able to teach and not be resentful. Verses 25 and 26 conveys the steps on how we can reach out to others to help them, but without gentleness the door may not be opened for us to do so.

Titus 3:2 states: "to slander no one, to be peaceable and considerate, and to show true humility toward all men". NIV. *The word "slander" is defined (S): "to vilify (to speak ill of; defame; slan-*

der); specifically to speak impiously (disrespectful)", and (Y): "to speak injuriously", and (D): "to speak harmful untruths about". This word, in the Greek, is "blasphemeo", where we get the word "blasphemy". **An alternate version: "to slander or abuse or speak evil of". AMP.**

Our first rule is not to vilify, that is to speak ill of another. We must not be disrespectful or speak harmful untruths about anyone. If we use these traits, we are in direct opposition to gentleness and alienate everyone around us.

The second word "peaceable" is defined (Y): "not fighting; not striving", and (D): "not in a noisy quarrel, squabble or fight". **An alternate version: "uncontentious", (not tending to arguments or strife). AMP.**

We are not to fight by argument, but to be peaceable, for when we fight against anyone, we step out of our fortitude or a defense. There is only one true enemy we are to fight, Satan, and not each other. All the fruit of the Spirit is used to help people and to fight against the true enemy, Satan.

The third word "considerate" is defined (S): "appropriate, that is (by implication) mild", and (Y): "yielding; pliant (bending easily; yielding; compliant)", **An alternate version: "to be forbearing (yielding, gentle and conciliatory)". AMP.**

We have found that the way we are to act toward each other is by being appropriate or fitting to the person and his situation. We are to be yielding or pliant, and not rigid, to the person in need, by being considerate of them; not resisting or opposing, but being open and flexible to the situation, where we would be useful to them and display our moral excellence in character or demeanor. When we do this, they will see that we are genuine and they will not build walls against us.

James 3:17 states: "But the wisdom that comes from heaven is first of all pure; then peace loving, considerate, submissive, full of mercy and good fruit, impartial and sincere". NIV. The word "wisdom" is defined (S): "wisdom (higher or lower; worldly or spiritual)", and (D): "knowledge of what is true or right coupled with just judgment as to action; sagacity; discernment; insight".

The word wisdom can be lower or higher, worldly or spiritual, but the wisdom that is stated here is the one that comes from God. We must, therefore, seek God's wisdom with all our being.

The first word "peace loving" is defined (S): "pacific (tending to make peace); by implication salutary (promoting or conducive to some beneficial benefit)".

One of the definitions for peace is prosperity found in Galatians 5:22. **Hebrews 12:14 states: "Make every effort to live in peace** with all men and to be holy; without holiness no one will see the Lord". NIV. It quotes here that we are to make every effort to live in peace with all men and to be holy (through the process of sanctification), in order where we can see the Lord. We must perceive that every aspect from God must work together, just like peace and gentleness.

The second word is "considerate", and is defined (S): "appropriate, that is (by implication) mild". We see that James is repeating what Paul said about gentleness/considerate in Titus 3:2. We know that two or three witnesses establishes the fact in the world, the same is true in Scriptures. If these two Holy Spirit inspired men, who wrote about gentleness/considerate, shouldn't we think it important, that we incorporate this in our lives daily?

The last word is "good fruit", and is defined (S): "fruit (as plucked), figuratively or literally". We see that fruit is what we are attaining for, looking to be the benefit to others from us, as well as we ourselves from others. The fruit we must have must come to maturity to be useful to use.

John 15:2,4-5,8 states: "He cuts off every branch in me that bears no fruit, while every branch that does bear fruit he trims clean so that it will be even more fruitful. ...Remain in me, and I will remain in you. No branch can bear fruit by itself; it must remain in the vine. Neither can you bear fruit unless you remain in me. I am the vine; you are the branches. If a man remains in me and I in him, he will bear much fruit; apart from me you can do nothing...This is to my Father's glory, that you bear much fruit, showing yourselves to be my disciples". NIV. We are to become very fruitful, for it is the will of God for us. This is done by the pruning of the dead branches in our lives that burdens us down and makes us inefficient. It is to the glory of the Father that we bear much fruit. Gentleness, therefore, a function of the fruit of the Spirit, must also bear much.

The last Scripture we will use is found in Philippians 4:5: "Let your gentleness be evident to all. The Lord is near". NIV. "Gentleness" in alternate versions: "forbearing spirit." NAS., and "unselfishness (considerateness; forbearing spirit)" AMP. Another reference: "mildness, patience, kindness, moderation, meekness and gentleness". DAKES.

We see that our gentleness or forbearing spirit must become known to all men, including our employers. **I Peter 2:18 states: "Slaves, submit yourselves to your masters with all respect, not only to those who are good and considerate, but also to those who are harsh".** NIV. We, as employees, are to be submissive to our employers, whether they are good and considerate, or harsh. We may not like our employers, yet it doesn't give us the excuse not to show submissive respect/gentleness. God will see our consistency in acting in gentleness, and in due time will promote us. The people at large, in this world, are looking for genuineness in any organization. Shouldn't we do this in our Christian walk, since this is sometimes the only Jesus they will ever see, by our actions?

Let's review gentleness, where we can implement this in our daily lives. Gentleness is being useful and being morally excellent in characteristic or demeanor. Dakes puts it: to be gentle, soft-spoken, kind, even-tempered, cultured and refined in character and conduct.

The three Hebrew boys demonstrated their gentleness by remaining faithful to God in their situation. They didn't fight against the king, but trusted God for their deliverance.

Wives must not be pushy or flashy, but allow the love of God to be demonstrated in the atmosphere of gentleness. Husbands, likewise, must honor their wives and not to put them down, whether in private or public. We must be compassionate to each other, not giving evil back for the evil done to us. We, by doing this, demonstrate moral excellence in character or demeanor.

We are to draw near to each other and not apart by quarrels and disputes, for we are not in competition against each other. We must be gentle, in other words, affable or pleasantly easy to talk to, friendly and showing warmth. When we demonstrate gentleness, unwanted walls will come down, where we may reach out to help others and develop trust.

We must not vilify or speak ill of another, nor fight by arguing, or we step out of our peace which is our fortified place and defense. We must apply ourselves where we are gentle, in other words, pliable, considerate and yielding to the needs of others.

We must decide to operate in God's wisdom found in His word, where we can truly demonstrate: peace loving, considerate and good fruit. Peace loving is being able to tend to make peace, thereby promoting a beneficial benefit. Considerate is being able to be appropriate and gentle. Good fruit is being able to show the outward result for our acts of gentleness by God's wisdom.

God wants us to be very fruitful for it brings glory to Him. He prunes away our dead branches in our lives, where we can develop more fruit and exhibit a better ability, the fruit of gentleness, even when people are unreasonable or harsh. These actions reinforce our souls to come in line with God's word and what He expects from us.

8

Goodness: the fifth step on the foundation of love

We have discovered that longsuffering is patient endurance, a great act, has great understanding, looks to calm down, not hasty or pushy, led by God's authority, able to correct, reprove, encourage without faultfinding, and is worn like clothes where all men can see.

Gentleness was discovered to be usefulness and has moral excellence in character or demeanor, as well as, affable or pleasantly easy to talk to, showing warmth and friendliness, appropriate, mild, yielding and pliant. These two are the functions of the fruit of the Spirit, where we can control our minds.

We proceed next to "goodness", which is defined (S): "goodness, that is virtue or beneficence", and (Dakes): "the states of being good, kind, virtuous, benevolent, generous and God-like in life and conduct". "Virtue" is defined (D): "moral excellence; righteousness; conformity of ones life and conduct to moral and ethical principles; inherent power to produce effects; potency". "Beneficence" is defined (D): "the doing of good; active goodness or kindness; charity".

Looking at goodness in this light, we must develop it where we come to know more about moral excellence or gentleness. Understanding the righteous nature within our spirit man, we can conform our lives and conduct to moral and ethical principles set by God's word. We can bring about the inherent power to produce effects with potency from our born-again spirits, and we will have no problems to believe we can do good. We now know we have goodness within ourselves, therefore what do we do with it to help others?

Psalms 23:6 states: "Surely goodness and love will follow me all the days of my life, and I dwell in the house of the Lord forever". NIV. *"Follow" is defined (S): "to run after (usually with hos-*

tile intent: figuratively (of time) gone by)", and (Y): "to pursue", and (D): "to go in pursuit of".

We must notice that goodness and love is in pursuit or chasing after us, for the sole purpose to overtake and fill our lives. It is not pursuing or chasing as if to sneak up on us, but openly with hostile and violent means trying to apprehend us. Anything that God offers to us is always for our benefit, therefore why are we trying to hide from it, as if it were to hurt us? When we realize this, then we can then violently or hostilely pursue others with this goodness and love, offering the benefits openly and unashamedly.

Psalm 31:19 states: "How great is your goodness, which you have stored up for those who fear you, which you bestow in the sight of men on those who take refuge in you". NIV. *The first word "stored up" is defined (S): "to hide (by covering over); by implication to hoard or reserve", and (D): "to put away for future use; store up".*

God's goodness has already been laid up for us who fear Him, therefore we are the candidates for which God's great goodness was stored up for. God hid or covered over His goodness not to conceal it from us, but to hoard or reserve it for the rightful owners—us. Let's go and claim what is already ours!

The second word "bestow" is defined (S): "to do or make (systematically and habitually), especially to practice", and (D): "elaborated (worked out with great care); embellished (to beautify by or as if by ornamentation); and to put to some use, apply".

We see God doing something for us, and following through to the finish, because we trust in Him. Men-at-large do not consistently follow through, yet we can develop consistent trust in God, who never fails to follow through in what He said He'll do for us. God systematically and habitually does His goodness towards us in an elaborate way, worked out with great care and embellished it for us, beautifying it ornamentally for our enjoyment. God bestows goodness in our lives, where we can put it to use. If He has done this for us, should we not do the same towards others who don't even know anything about God's goodness? When God planted goodness into our hearts, He also gave us the ability to use it to help others.

Psalm 107:9 states: "for he satisfies the thirsty and fills the hungry with good things". NIV. *"Satisfies" is defined (S): "to sate (to satisfy any appetite or desire fully; glut), that is fill to satisfaction (literally and figuratively)", and (D): "the act of putting an end to (a desire, want, need etc.) by sufficient and ample provision". "Thirsty" is defined (S): "to course (like a beast of prey); by implication to seek*

Goodness: the fifth step on the foundation of love

greedily", and (Y): "to run to and fro", and (D): "to have an earnest or strong desire; yearn; eagerly desirous; craving".

God wants to satisfy the thirsty and He can only satisfy those who have an appetite or desire. God desires to actively put an end to the desire, want, need etc. by sufficient or ample provision. We, who believe, should be searching greedily for this sufficient and ample provision. We, just like the beast seeking for his prey, must seek for this provision, and must pursue it with an earnest and eager desire, otherwise, no matter how much God wants to provide, we will not receive.

The second part of this verse, "fills" is defined (S): "to fill or (intransitive) be full in a wide application (literally or figuratively)", and (D): "to supply to an extreme degree or plentifully". "Hungry" is defined (S): "to hunger", and (D): "a strong or compelling desire or craving".

God presents here the view of filling the hungry with the supply in an extreme degree or plentifully, yet God will not arbitrarily give anything without the one having a strong, or compelling desire, or craving for His goodness. When we give to someone, yet they don't want it or refuse to take it, doesn't it make us feel dejected? Imagine how God feels when we, who really need any and everything from God, don't eagerly, with strong, or compelling desire, or craving, apprehend it for ourselves. If we don't possess what rightfully belongs to us first, we cannot offer it to others. Get the picture? We must have it first in our lives operating before we can offer it to others to use.

Our last Scripture on "goodness" is found in Romans 2:4: "Or do you show contempt for the riches of his kindness, tolerance and patience, not realizing that God's kindness leads you towards repentance?". NIV. We will look at this in the perspective of how goodness stems out from gentleness. Goodness is sharp and active in comparison with gentleness which is mellow in context, yet goodness needs gentleness to express itself in its fullest form.

"Contempt" is defined (S): "to think against, that is disesteem", and (Y): " to think down upon", and (D): "to regard with contempt, disgust or disdain; scorn". "Riches" is defined (S): "wealth (as fullness), that is (literally) money possessions, or (figuratively) abundance, richness, (specifically) valuable bestowment". **An alternate version: "or are you (so blind as to) trifle with and presume upon and despise and underestimate...". AMP.**

We should see and understand that God is setting a strict standard, where we are not to despise or think against anything God has to offer to us. If we decide this, we automatically separate ourselves from fellowship with God, for He doesn't allow acts of contempt, distaste, disgust or disdain, and still keep fellowship with Him.

Many Christians think they are humble when they reject or despise owning anything of value, which is diametrically opposite of what God desires for us. Our earthly fathers desire the best for us, therefore what makes us believe that our Heavenly Father would act differently by taking away or preventing anything good, which include material things, to come to us? God is constantly looking to give us riches for our whole person (spirit, soul, body, social, financial), and He desires, through his children, to demonstrate that He is a God of plenty and not a God of lack or bearly getting by. God intends for us believers to have authority to possess riches, instead of those in this sinful world. If God intends this for us, shouldn't we believe He will provide a way for us to use these riches correctly?

God has many Scriptural reference of His richness towards us: **Romans 9:23: "What if he did this to make the riches of his glory known to the objects of his mercy...". NIV. Romans 11:33: "Oh, the depth of the riches of the wisdom and knowledge of God". NIV. Ephesians 1:7, 1:18, 2:7, 3:8: "In him we have redemption through his blood, the forgiveness of sins, in accordance with the riches of God's grace...I pray also that the eyes of your heart may be enlightened in order that you may know the hope to which he has called you, the riches of his glorious inheritance in the saints...in order that in the coming ages he might show the incomparable riches of his grace, expressed in his kindness to us in Christ Jesus...to preach to the Gentiles the unsearchable riches of Christ". NIV. Philippians 4:19: "And my God will meet all your needs according to his glorious riches in Christ Jesus". NIV. Colossians 2:2: "My purpose is that they may be encouraged in heart and united in love, so that they may have the full riches of complete understanding...". NIV.** We can see that God wants richness in all areas of our lives, therefore let's not deny any.

"Kindness " is defined (S): "usefulness, excellence in moral character or demeanor", and (Y): "usefulness; benignity (quality of being kindly disposed; good deed or favor)".

We are not to show contempt for the richness from God's goodness, or good deed, favor and kindness towards us. We must esteem or admire the goodness or kindness of God as a valuable bestowment upon us, therefore we must apprehend it for our use and present it to others, that they may know and receive.

The second section of the verse, the word "leads" is defined (S): "to lead; by implication to bring, drive, or (figuratively) induce". "Repentance" is defined (S): "compunction (a feeling of uneasiness or anxiety of the conscience caused by regret for doing wrong or pain);

Goodness: the fifth step on the foundation of love 49

by implication reversal (of another's decision)", and (D): "to feel such sorrow for sin or fault as to be disposed to change one's life for the better". **An alternate version: "(to change your mind and inner man to accept God's will)". AMP.**

We can now see the greater value of the goodness offered to us. Goodness or kindness leads us to repentance. We, as believers, must repent of our shortcomings in this life, that we may remain humble, yet not self-debasing, before God, therefore receiving the goodness or kindness of God richly. Repentance is not begging God to forgive, but believing God has totally forgiven, therefore never bringing it up again and insulting Him. Repentance is for the present situation or sin, where we can remain in constant fellowship with God.

Now if you have never accepted and received the redemptive work of Jesus on the cross of Calvary, all your sins are still with you. When you decide to accept and receive, then all your sins are forgiven and washed away. You then have a completely clean slate, and have complete relationship and fellowship with God. So what are you waiting for? Come and join the family which has far greater benefits than the world can offer.

Let's review goodness. We found that goodness or kindness is moral excellence in an active mode, thereby being God-like in life and conduct. Goodness has within it the inherent power to produce effects with potency.

Goodness or kindness is running after us as in pursuit to overcome and fill our lives, therefore we must not hide, but get into position to be violently and hostily overtaken and filled. We will then be able to violently and hostily pursue others with this same goodness or kindness, offering the benefits openly and unashamedly.

Goodness or kindness was laid up for us, in other words, God hid it for us and not from us, therefore it rightfully belongs to us. Goodness or kindness was also elaborated or worked out with great care, and embellished or beautifully ornamented, where we can put it to some good use.

We must have an appetite or desire to be satisfied, where the end to the desire, want or need is thoroughly provided sufficiently and amply. We must have the strong and compelling desire or craving supplied to an extreme degree and with plenitude. God desires to supply His goodness or kindness to us, in turn, we can share it with others who don't know about God's goodness or kindness.

We are not to despise or think against anything God offers to us, for it has great value for our use and enjoyment. We must not reject God's goodness or kindness, which is of great value, thinking it produces humbleness. Humbleness is proven when we totally rely on God in every area of our lives (spirit, soul, body, financial, social), whether with or without possessions.

God's goodness or kindness, when active in our lives, leads us to repentance. Repentance is not degrading ourselves, but being humble before God and turning away from sin, therefore being in position to receive. A reminder, once our sins are forgiven by faith, we must not bring up that sin again, thereby insulting God.

Love, joy and peace covers the area of the spirit man, giving it a platform to work from, which is a direct relationship with God. Longsuffering, gentleness and goodness covers the area of the soul (will, emotion and intellect) to think in line with the word of God, and it originates in our spirit man. We can, with these, see God from the perspective of our soul, which works in our lives to understand others and how to minister to them. The first three shows us how we are to relate with God from our spirit man, therefore reaching out to others. The second three shows us, from our souls, how we relate with others around us. The third three will show us, from our physical bodies, how we are to relate with ourselves in controlling our nature to do what the spirit man desires, and in turn showing others.

9

Faith: the sixth step on the foundation of love

We found in the previous chapter that goodness is moral excellence in action and is running after us as in pursuit to overcome us. God hid goodness for us and not from us, therefore we must have an appetite for satisfaction and a hunger to be filled with goodness. We are not to despise or think down on God's goodness thinking we are humble in doing so. Goodness leads us to repentance. Goodness, together with longsuffering and gentleness, functions from our spirit man through our souls where we can relate with others around us.

The seventh function of the fruit of the Spirit is "faith", defined (S): "persuasion (to prevail on a person to do something, as by advising; urging), that is credence (belief as to the truth of something); moral conviction (act of believing in the truth of what is alleged) of the truthfulness of God or religious teacher or religious truth)" and (Y): 'faith, faithfulness, steadfastness". An alternate reference: "the living, divinely implanted, acquired and created principle of inward and wholehearted confidence, assurance, trust and reliance in God and all He says". DAKES. **Alternate versions: "faithfulness". NIV. NASB. AMP.**

The word "faith" is defined (D): "confidence or trust in a person or thing", and "faithfulness" (D): "strict or thorough in the performance of duty, in other words, implies long-continued and steadfast fidelity to whatever one is bound to by a pledge, duty or obligation; steady in allegiance or affection".

God is looking for people who will stay constant through any situation whether good or bad. A tree for example, doesn't change its fruit because the weather wasn't totally conducive to the tree, but the tree does its best to produce the fruit in spite of the conditions. Therefore we must be steadfast and faithful to ourselves in any and all circumstances. If we don't remain faithful to ourselves we will never remain faithful towards God and others. Faith and faithfulness operates through the realm of our body/flesh. These are produced in our spirit man, but it operates (or functions) through our fleshly bodies, thereby putting a physical proof in what we believe, just like God said, "We prove our love for God by loving others". We prove our faithfulness towards God and others by being faithful to ourselves first.

The first Scripture is found in Hebrews 11:1 "Now faith is being sure of what we hope for and certain of what we do not see". NIV. *"Faith"* is defined (S): *"persuasion, credence, moral conviction, reliance and constancy"*. Faith in this light proves it must be accompanied by action on our part for it to be alive in our lives which is faithfulness.

"Being sure of" is defined (S): *"a setting under (support), that is (figuratively) concretely essence (the basic, real and invariable nature of the thing), or abstract assurance (full confidence; freedom from doubt; certainty)"*, and (Y): *"what stands under, substration (something which underlies or serves as a basis or foundation)"*. **An alternate version: "assurance (the confirmation, title deed)". AMP.** An alternate reference: *"support, ground work, confidence, subsistence, reality. Used in the papyrus of title deeds"*. DAKES.

Faith has substance, and it is not inanimate, but has a support, essence and an assurance. **God said in Hebrews 11:6 "And without faith it is impossible to please God, because anyone who comes to him must believe that he exist and that he rewards those who earnestly seek him". NIV.** God made provisions for us to obtain faith and we must learn to use it faithfully. Faith has a basic, real and invariable nature, therefore we can rely on its constancy, like a foundation. Real estate land, for example, is basic, real and invariable, therefore a title deed can be obtained and solidify ownership. God set up for us, the same way, where we can obtain faith as a title deed and solidify our ownership. When faith becomes our own property, we will become faithful to it, like the land-owner is to his real estate property. Faith is not some mysterious idea and it is not blind, therefore we must not loose sight of it, but become faithful to receive the benefits.

How does faith work for us? **Luke 17:5-10 states: "The apostles said to the Lord, 'Increase our faith!' He replied, 'If you have faith as small as a mustard seed, you can say to this mulberry tree, 'Be uprooted and planted in the sea', and it will obey you. Suppose one of you had a servant plowing or looking after the sheep. Would he say to the servant when he comes in from the field, 'Come along now and sit down to eat'? Would he not rather say, 'prepare my supper, get yourself ready and**

Faith: the sixth step on the foundation of love

wait on me while I eat and drink; after that you may eat and drink'? Would he thank the servant because he did what he was told to do? So you also, when you have done everything you were told to do, should say, 'We are unworthy servants; we have only done our duty'." NIV.

We have, here, a story about the apostles asking for more faith, yet Jesus didn't give them more, but showed them how to use what they already had. Faith has already been implanted in us when we become Christians, therefore we must learn how to use it. Let's look at the Bible, the owners' manual for life, on how we can learn to use faith properly, thereby being faithful.

The first word "increase" is defined (S): "to place additionally, that is lay beside, annex, repeat", and (Y): "to put towards, add to", and (D): "to make greater in any respect; augment; add to".

We see that the apostles were looking to add to their faith, that is, place additionally, lay beside and annex to their current faith. When we use our muscles, do we increase in the number of muscles or the strength? We maintain our muscles at peak performance, when we exercise it consistently or faithfully, and the same is true with our faith. Therefore we must learn to develop or exercise faith were strength will result. This is what Jesus wanted the disciples to learn, therefore He proceeded to explain how faith works.

We find in verse 6: "...If you have faith as small as a mustard seed, you can SAY ...and it will OBEY you". The first word "say" is defined (S): "to lay forth, that is (figuratively) relate (in words (usually of systematically or set discourse))", and (Y): "to say, speak, lay out".

We must actively develop our muscles by prescribed plans of exercise, therefore we must actively develop our faith by prescribed plans of exercise through God's word. We are not to babble just anything, but must have all our words prepared ahead of time. We must lay forth or relate in words, usually in a systematic or set discourse, on what we desire. This means, we must do some research on what God says, for us to develop our faith to faithfulness.

The second word "obey" is defined (D): "to hear under (as a subordinate), that is to listen attentively; by implication to heed or conform to a command or authority", and (Y): "to hearken submissively".

What we say, whether good or evil, must obey or subordinate itself to us, therefore our words should be lining up to what we desire. Faith must heed or conform to our command or authority, therefore our words must line up to what we desire. The wrong exercises performed will not get the desired results, therefore our words wrongly spoken will also not get the desired results. The results, just like faithfulness, always subordinate or hearken submissively to what has been said. Our intent is not good enough, but our right words said is needed for the desired results to be subordinate to its commands or authority. God's word is the best and only source for the right results needed for our daily lives.

Jesus continues, in verses 7 through 10, where He shows how a servant serves his master, as a duty under his command or authority, therefore he has no legal choice but to obey him in a subordinate position. When we serve and obey God, God will delegate to us, where we can release our faith as a servant to obey us. Will we release our faith to do the word of the world which leads to loss and destruction, or the words of God which leads to gain, success and life to God's glory? God had said, "we choose!"

The next Scripture is Matthew 13:31-32: "He told them another parable: 'The kingdom of heaven is like a mustard seed, which a man took and planted in his field. Though it is the smallest of all your seeds, yet when it grows, it is the largest of garden plants and becomes a tree, so that the birds of the air come and perch in its branches'". NIV.
We will look at two words: "took and planted". *The first word "took" is defined (S): "to take; (properly objective or active), to get hold of", and (D): "to get into one's hold or possession by voluntary action". The second word "planted" is defined (S): "to scatter; that is sow (literally or figuratively)", and (D): "to scatter seed for the purpose of growth".*

This seed, which is God's word, must be taken into our hold or possession by our voluntary action, for it will not just fall on us. We must take action to take hold of it, and must follow through by planting it in the field, an analogy of our hearts. All these actions demonstrate an outward expression of our faith within, and as we follow through, we develop faithfulness from the word planted. The mustard seed produces a mustard tree and becomes useful for food and lodging, therefore when we plant the seed derived from God's word, we produce faithfulness useful for our use. Faith is not static but active, because we must take and plant the word into our hearts, thereby producing faithfulness.

The last Scripture is Romans 10:17: "Consequently, faith comes from hearing the message, and the message is heard through the word of Christ". NIV. *The word "hearing" is defined (S): "hearing (the act, the sense or the thing heard)", and (D): "to listen to; give or pay attention to".*

Faith comes into being by listening or hearing the word of God, which is the carrier of the seed of faith. The word of God is a container, which contains the directive, faith and anointing (power to carry out the

Faith: the sixth step on the foundation of love

directive). Our words are containers also, therefore we must align our words with God's word, to obtain the same purpose. When we continually hear the word of God, we build up our faith capacity, where we have the directives in the word come about. The anointing or power to execute will back up our action, thereby proving our faithfulness. We cannot just listen once or twice and expect great results, for we have not developed any faithfulness to the word. We must listen or hear continually for faith to develop stronger and stronger. When faith is not operating, it will wane, just like muscles when not used, will wane until atrophy sets in.

Let's review faith, where we discovered that it is a persuasion, credence, moral conviction, reliance and constancy. Faith must be accompanied by actions, which include our physical bodies, to be real in our lives.

Faith has substance, therefore it is a support, essence and an assurance. We, to please God, must be in faith. Real estate property must have a title deed, just like faith must have a title deed, to solidify ownership. Faith is not a mysterious idea and it is not blind, but is basic, real and invariable, therefore we must develop it to faithfulness to reap the benefits.

Faith has been put into us when we become born-again or believers, therefore we must not ask God for it or ask for more. Muscles must be used to be developed, and the same is true for faith. We develop faith by speaking it out, and the words we use determine what kind of faith we develop. Faith is our servant and will do what we tell it to do, therefore we must prepare what to say to obtain the desired result. If we are not getting the results we desire, we must check the words we are using. God is always desiring good for us, therefore, it is reasonable to use His proven words for our faith to subordinate to, to get the desired results.

We as man (male or female) must take the word into our possession willingly, for it will not fall on us or force itself on us. We must plant it into our hearts by speaking it out. These outward actions demonstrate our faith within, because seeds planted will grow, just as words planted will grow. When it matures, it will produce faithfulness in our lives.

Words are containers having in it the directive, faith and anointing. We must continually plant the word into our hearts and release it by faith for it to work. Then the anointing will give it the power to carry out the directive. We, by hearing the word continually, plant it into our hearts until our faith builds up the capacity to perform it fully, thereby proving our faithfulness.

We see, that faith depends on our physical body to carry out the desired result, thereby proving faithfulness. This function of the fruit of the Spirit deals with our physical body, for God is interested in our whole being (spirit, soul and body).

10

Meekness: the seventh step on the foundation of love

We discovered, in the previous chapter, that faith has substance and is not inanimate. Real estate have title deeds to solidify ownership, and needs to be developed to increase value. Faith, also, has a title deed to solidify ownership, and needs to be developed to increase value to faithfulness. Words determine the kind of faith developed, therefore we must choose carefully the right words because faith, as our servant, responds to our words, to its desired end result. We must apprehend the word voluntarily and plant it into our hearts, by speaking it out. Words we plant will grow and mature producing faithfulness, whether good or evil. The more often we speak out the word, the more word gets planted within, making the directives clearer, faith stronger, and more power available to carry out the directives, which develops faithfulness.

The eighth function of the fruit of the Spirit is "meekness", defined (S): "gentleness, by implication humility", and (Y): "meekness, mildness", and (D): "humbly patient or submissive". **Alternate versions: "gentleness" NIV. NASB., and "gentleness (meekness, humility)". AMP.** *An alternate reference: "the disposition to be gentle, kind, indulgent (kindly disposed and gracious), even balanced in tempers and passions, and patient in suffering injuries without feeling a spirit of rage". DAKES.*

Meekness is defined as gentleness, humility and submission, and these qualities are not a sign of weakness, but of great fortitude. Meekness is not being weak and useless, and attributed to those classified as losers in society. The more we humble ourselves, or act meek before God, the more God will lift us up in due time. **I Peter 5:5-6, states: "Clothe yourselves with humility toward one another, because, 'God opposes the proud but gives grace to the humble'. Humble yourselves, therefore, under God's mighty hand, that**

Meekness: the seventh step on the foundation of love

he may lift you up in due time". NIV. The more we submit to others, the more we will win them to our side. **I Corinthians 9:19 states: "'Though I am free and belong to no man, I make myself a slave to everyone, to win as many as possible". NIV.**

Our first Scripture on "meekness" is found in **Psalms 25:9: "He guides the humble in what is right and teaches them his way". NIV.** *Our subject word "humble" is defined (S): "depressed (figuratively), in mind (gentle) or circumstances (needy)", and (Y): "humble". An alternate reference: "those who acknowledge that they are without resources in themselves".* NIV STUDY BIBLE.

The term meekness/meek is synonymous with humility/humble. Meekness/humility is not the degrading of ourselves, so that we portray this degradation of ourselves in front of others. This degrading action will also be portrayed in front of God, yet He never asked us to degrade but to submit ourselves to Him, where He can move on our behalf. God requires of us this attribute of meekness/humility, therefore He gives us the ability to accomplish it. We have meekness/humility planted into us when we accept and receive the redemptive work of Jesus on our behalf, therefore we are already meek/humble. We just need to develop it, where it can function properly.

The second word "guides" is defined (S): "to tread; by implication to walk", and (Y): "to cause to tread (to form by action of walking; path)", and (D): "to assist; in an area in which he does not know the way; accompanying him to show points of interest and to explain their meaning or significance".

We see that one of the benefits of meekness/humility is guidance. When we decide to operate in this, we put aside our way of doing things and submit to God's guidance. God will walk or tread with us to assist in areas we don't know, showing points of interest and explaining the meaning or significance. All we need to do is to operate in meekness/humility, and God will have a clear path to show us to any and all answers we inquire of from Him.

The third word "what is right" is defined (S): "verdict (favorable or unfavorable) pronounced judicially; justice", and (D): "the ability to judge, make a decision, or form an opinion objectively, authoritatively, and wisely especially in matters affecting action; good sense; discretion".

Meekness/humility puts us in position for God to work in our lives. When we submit to God, He can guide or tread with us in areas we don't know. He will show us points of interest and explain the meaning or significance, therefore coming up with a verdict, pronounced judicially. We then can have the ability to judge, make a decision, or form an opinion objectively, authoritatively and wisely especially in matters affecting action, good sense and discretion. When we demonstrate meekness/humility God's way, we get lifted up in what is right, thereby becoming stronger and not weaker.

The next word "teaches" is defined (S): "to goad, that is (by implication) to teach (the rod being an oriental incentive)", and (Y): "to teach (in an active sense as if violently)", and (D): "instruct, tutor, educate, inform, enlighten, discipline, train, drill, school, indoctrinate". The word "way" is defined (S): "a road (as trodden); figuratively a course of life or mode of action", and (Y): "trodden path or way". The words "guides" and "way" come from the same root word in Hebrew.

God wants to teach us His way, as we decide to be meek/humble before God. God's form of teaching is as if goading, that is to drive us or in an active sense as if violently. The enemy, Satan, is ever driving against us to lead us away, but God teaches us to lead us to him for our good. God wants to teach or goad us to His way, a road trodden in a course of life or mode of action, proven for our good. Teaching is described as a rod, being an oriental incentive, which may seem rather harsh on the surface, but let's look at where God said that discipline is for our good. **Hebrews 12:5-11 addresses this issue: "And you have forgotten the word of encouragement that addresses you as sons: 'My son, do not make light of the Lord's discipline, and do not lose heart when he rebukes you, because the Lord disciplines those he loves, and he punishes everyone he accepts as a son'. Endure hardship as discipline; God is treating you as sons. For what son is not disciplined by his father? If you are not disciplined (and everyone undergoes discipline), then you are illegitimate children and not true sons. Moreover, we have all had human fathers who disciplines us and we respected them for it. How much more should we submit to the Father of our spirits and live! Our fathers disciplined us for a little while as they thought best; but God disciplines us for our good, that we may share in his holiness. No discipline seems pleasant at the time, but painful. Later on, however, it produces a harvest of righteousness and peace for those who have been trained by it". NIV**. Meekness, to sum it up, is the given ability to willingly submit under a higher authority, which is in this case God, who will supply what is lacking in us, as God deems beneficial for us.

The next Scripture is found in **Psalms 37:11: "But the meek will inherit the land and enjoy great peace". NIV.** The commentary of the word "meek" is : "those who humbly acknowledge their dependence on the goodness and grace of God, and betray no arrogance toward their fellow man". NIV Study Bible. The word "inherit" is defined (S): "to occupy (by driving out previous tenants, and possessing in their place)", and (Y): "to occupy, possess", and (D): "to take or receive (property, a right, a title, etc.) by succession or will". The word "land" is defined (S): "to be firm; the earth (at large, or partitive a land)", and (Y): "earth, land".

We, the meek/humble, have been given great authority, and the right of inheritance. We must occupy and possess by driving out the previous tenants, the devil and his cohorts operating through ungodly men. We must not betray arrogance toward a fellow man by stealing what rightfully belongs to him. We must take back what rightfully belongs to us as an inheritance, which was stolen from us.

The devil apprehended by deception from Adam, his rightful inheritance, when he fell. Adam, though deceived, willingly gave it up. When Jesus rose from the dead, He took it back from the devil. Then He gave the inheritance back to us, to those who decide to accept and receive the redemptive work of Jesus for ourselves. If it belongs to us, let's take possession and drive the devil out.

The second part of this Scripture reflect the benefits of this inheritance. *The word "enjoy" is defined (S): "to be soft or pliable, that is (figuratively) effeminate or luxurious", and (Y): "to delight self in a reflective way", and (D): "to give great pleasure, satisfaction or enjoyment to; please highly".*

The meek/humble are to enjoy and not be in somber gloom and despair. When we enjoy, we are not stiff or rigid, but soft and pliable, where enjoying can reflect back on us. Doesn't it seem good to us to give pleasure, satisfaction or enjoyment to others, in turn receiving back the same? Now what are we to enjoy or delight in?

The word "great" is defined (S): "'abundance (in any respect)", and (Y): "abundance, multitude", and (D): "an extremely plentiful or oversufficient quantity or supply". The word "peace" is defined (S): "safe, that is (figuratively) well, happy, friendly; welfare, that is health, prosperity, peace", and (Y): "peace, completeness".

We, being meek/humble, have considerable and profound benefits at our disposal. If we as parents desire the best for our children, shouldn't we think that God, the perfect Father, would desire it more for His children? We, as meek/humble before God, then can enjoy or delight in abundance. Most people's idea of meek/humble is to be without and be in constant lack, yet God never desired this for us. God desires to be lavish or luxurious with us since we are His children. What kind of abundance does God desire for us?

God's desire for us is peace, defined as safe, well, happy and friendly. God's abundance doesn't just cover one part of our lives but all of it since God is interested in our welfare in health, prosperity and peace. He takes interest in our receiving these abundantly. Let's receive these in enjoyment with a meek/ humble heart and attitude. A commentary states: "unmixed blessedness, and the Hebrew word 'shalom' is seen in its most expressive fullness-not the absence of war, but a positive state of rightness, and well being which can only come from the Lord". NIV Study Bible.

The following Scripture in Matthew 5:5 states: "Blessed are the meek, for they will inherit the earth". NIV. *The word "blessed"' is defined (S): "supremely blest; by extension fortunate, well-off", and (Y): "happy", and (D): "divinely or supremely favored; fortunate...blissfully happy or contented".* **An alternate version: "(happy, blithesome, joyous, spiritually prosperous—with life joy and satisfaction in God's favor and salvation, regardless of their outward conditions". AMP.**

The word "meek" comes from the same root word in Greek for meekness. A commentary states: "mild-tempered, gentle spirit". Dakes.

We, as the meek/humble, must demonstrate a gentle spirit and mild temperance before God as well as before man. When we stand in this position we are blessed, and it is permanent if we stay in this position, since it is supremely conditioned, resulting in being fortunate and well off, or divinely or supremely favored; blissfully happy or contented. We, on account of this, no longer need to ever be anxious about the outward situations, for we are, with life joy and satisfaction, in God's favor and salvation. What are the benefits of being blessed?

The word "inherit" is defined (S): "to be an heir (literally and figuratively)", a root word used as a noun: "sharer by lot, that is an inheritor (literally or figuratively); by implication a possessor", and (Y): "to obtain by lot".

We, as meek/humble before God and man, are blessed with no regard to outward conditions, and know that we have an inheritance that rightfully belongs to us. God is the provider of our inheritance, therefore we can be assured fully or blessed that it will always be there, and never run out of its limitless assets. We, as we continue our study on meekness, discover more benefits that are accrued to us, giving us the incentive to remain meek/humble, and demonstrating it by the results we obtain. We must continue in these to produce meekness/humility, which is a function of the fruit of the Spirit, for it has great value.

Our final Scripture on "meekness" is found in I Peter 3:4: "Instead, it should be that of your inner self, the unfading beauty of a gentle and quiet spirit, which is of great worth in God's sight". NIV.

Meekness: the seventh step on the foundation of love

The phrase *"inner self"* is defined (S): *"concealed, that is private"*. **An alternate version: "the inward adorning and beauty of the hidden man". AMP.** This is definitely speaking about our spirit man hidden from view of our natural eyes. **Scriptural proof is found in Romans 7:22: "For in my inner being I delight in God's law;". NIV.**

The phrase *"unfading beauty"* is defined (S): *"undecaying (in essence or continuance)* and (Y): *"incorruptible"*, and (D): *"not debased in character; not depraved or perverted; morally upright (righteous)"*. **Alternate versions: "imperishable quality", NAS., and "incorruptible and unfading charm". AMP.**

Our inner self or spirit man must operate in an unfading beauty or righteous in character, therefore knowing how to live as meek/humble in spirit. Meekness/humility brings out the incorruptible, unfading beauty, and imperishable quality of character within our spirit man.

The phrase *"gentle and quiet spirit"* comes next. The word *"quiet"* is defined (S): *"properly keeping one's seat (sedentary), that is (by implication) still (undisturbed, undisturbing)"*, And (Y): *"mild, tranquil, gentle"*, and (D): *"free from disturbance or turmoil; tranquil; peaceful"*. **An alternate version: "peaceful (not anxious or wrought up)". AMP.** An additional reference: *"meekness, so as not to be provoked by others, and a quiet spirit, so as not to provoke others"*. DAKES.

Our inner self or spirit man must operate in an unfading beauty or righteous in character, therefore being meek/humble and quiet in spirit. A quiet spirit has the ability to stay seated in an undisturbed state, and is not anxious or wrought up by outside situations that are trying to crowd in. Meekness controls us from being provoked by others, while quietness controls us from being provoking to others.

The last phrase *"great worth"* is defined (S): *"extremely expensive"*, and (Y): *"very expensive"*, and (D): *"that which must be given, done and/or undergone in order to obtain a thing"*.

Our gentle and quiet spirit, in God's sight, was extremely expensive to obtain, therefore it has great worth. God had to give His Son, Jesus, where He could undergo death for our sins, and rise from the grave to obtain for us life, is compared to the dictionary definition: *"that which must be given, done, and/or undergone in order to obtain a thing"*. Therefore, what was needed in order to obtain man back must be of great worth. It is reasonable, then, that we must operate in a meek/humble and quiet/ undisturbed heart, where we are kept in an unfading beauty or righteous in character.

We have come to the conclusion on what meekness is and how it effects our lives. Let's review, so that we can assimilate and put in practice and receive its benefits. Meekness is defined as gentleness, by implication humility, and is not a sign of weakness but of great fortitude, and in its truest sense brings exaltation from God.

Meekness was planted in us, therefore God gave us the ability to carry it out. We must exercise it to the point of functioning properly. Meekness is not degrading ourselves but submitting to God, where He can move on our behalf.

Meekness provides guidance, where we put aside our way of doing things, and submit to God's way. God will guide us in areas unknown to us, showing points of interest, and explaining the meanings and significance. Once we get to this point we have the ability to judge, make a decision, or form an opinion objectively, authoritatively, and wisely especially in matters affecting action, good sense and discretion.

Meekness brings God on the scene to teach us His ways. His teaching is a form of goading or driving us His way, a road trodden, in a course of life or mode of action, proven for our good. This is done as an incentive which may seem harsh on the surface, but it is very beneficial for our growth, just as discipline is for our children.

Meekness has great authority given it, the right of inheritance, where we drive out the previous tenants (the devil), and possess it in his place. We don't betray arrogance against anyone by taking what belongs to them, but we take back what was stolen from us. Adam gave the right of inheritance to the devil when he fell, but Jesus, when He rose from the grave, took it back and gave it to those who decide to believe (not all of mankind). Let's take our rightful inheritance.

Meekness is to enjoy and not be somber, gloomy or in despair, therefore we are soft and pliable, where it reflects back on us. Let's enjoy meekness for it is more satisfying, gives more pleasure, and has greater enjoyment for others as well as for ourselves When meekness operates, we gain abundance, unlike the world's perception of lack and doing without. God wants us to be lavished and in luxury, therefore having the ability to help others. God's abundance include peace, safety, well-being, happiness and friendship, and it produces health, prosperity and peace in our lives.

Meekness attributes gentleness of spirit and mild temperance, and we are called blessed, resulting in a supreme condition of being fortunate and well-off. We need never be anxious, but be with life, joy and satisfaction in God's favor and salvation. God is the provider of our inheritance, therefore we are fully assured and blessed to know, that it will not run out of its unlimited supply.

Our inner-self or spirit men must operate in an unfading beauty or righteous in character, so that we have a quiet and gentle spirit. Meekness controls us from being provoked by others, while quietness controls us from being provoking to others. God paid an expensive price to redeem us, therefore we are of great worth to Him.

Meekness operates through our flesh bodies, but originates in our spirit man. It regulates our flesh bodies to submit to God's way, thereby moving us towards the right results and goals, what God intended for our good and benefit. Faith needs our flesh bodies to carry out faith, thereby producing faithfulness, therefore meek/humble needs our flesh bodies to carry out meek/humble, thereby producing meekness/humility.

11

Temperance: the eighth step on the foundation of love

We found, in the previous chapter, that meekness/humility was not a sign of weakness, but of great fortitude, and it does not degrade itself. Meekness provides guidance in areas unknown providing meanings and significance, where we can judge, decide and form an opinion objectively, authoritatively and wisely. It teaches God's way, goading or disciplining us onto the trodden road, proven for our good. It has great authority given, the right of inheritance, where we take back possession by driving out the previous tenants, the devil. God desires the best for us, His children; which include health, prosperity and peace. Our inner self or spirit man must operate in unfading beauty or righteous in character. A meek spirit controls against being provoked by others, while a quiet spirit controls against being provoking to others.

Let's proceed to the word "temperance", defined (S): "self-controlled (especially continence (self-restraint in regard to sexual passion or activity))", and (Y): "self-restraint, continence", and (D): "to habitually moderate or self-restrain in the indulgences of the natural appetites and passions".

What is the most troublesome part of man? It is, of course, our flesh bodies, which is ever trying to have complete control. God knew this, therefore He gave us the function of the fruit of the Spirit called temperance/self-control, yet without the previous eight, this one will not work properly in any lasting fashion. Temperance/self-control involves direct actions on our part. We must develop a habit in temperance/self-control to have the ability to moderate or self-restrain the over-indulgence of our natural appetites or passions. The natural appetites or passions are not

Temperance: the eighth step on the foundation of love 65

evil in themselves, but the uncontrolled use of these. Natural appetites and passions are needed to live, but it is the over-indulgence that causes the flesh to wear out prematurely, which in God's sight is evil and sinful.

The first Scripture is found in I Corinthians 9:25a: "Everyone who competes in the games goes into strict training". NIV. *The word "compete" is defined (S): "to struggle, literally (to compete for a prize), figuratively (to contend with an adversary), or generally (to endeavor to accomplish something)", And (Y): "to agonize, contend", and (D): "to exert oneself vigorously; try hard; to make strenuous efforts towards a goal; to contend in opposition, battle or any conflict; compete; to struggle vigorously, as in opposition or resistance". The second phrase "goes into strict training" is defined (S): "to exercise self-restraint (in diet and chastity)", and (Y): "to be self-restrained, continence".*

We must compete to gain the benefits of temperance by setting goals to attain the results. These goals must have pressure placed on them, like competing in the games to obtain the prize, which is the reward for doing so. This striving or contention is with our flesh bodies, and not the devil. We Christians too often don't exert pressure against our flesh bodies by going into strict training to gain control and victory.

God knew that we would have difficulties with our rebellious flesh bodies, therefore He implanted temperance within our hearts. When we exercise in temperance/self-control, we will in strict training regulate our flesh body to do what it was designed to do. We will no longer struggle needlessly, because our flesh bodies will no longer have dominance. We, not anyone else including God, must exercise in temperance/self-control. **An alternate version of this Scripture is: "And everyone who competes in the games exercises self-control in all things". NASB.**

The next Scripture, II Peter 1:5-10 is: "For this very reason, make every effort to add to your faith goodness; and to goodness knowledge; and to knowledge self-control; and to self-control perseverance; and to perseverance godliness; and to godliness brotherly kindness; and to brotherly kindness love. For if you possess these qualities in increasing measure, they will keep you from being ineffective and unproductive in your knowledge of our Lord Jesus Christ. But if anyone does not have them, he is nearsighted and blind, and has forgotten that he has been cleansed from his past sins. Therefore, my brothers, be all the more eager to make your calling and election sure. For if you do these things, you will never fall,". NIV.

We will find, in this Scripture, many words previously covered. They tie together including temperance/self-control, drawing from each other to reach the intended goals and results.

The first phrase "make every effort" is defined (S): "to bear alongside, that is introduce simultaneously...speed, that is (by implication) dispatch, eagerness, earnestness", and (Y): "to bear into beside...haste speed,", and (D): "to make, do or perform... constant effort to accomplish what is undertaken; persistent exertion of body and mind". **An alternate version: "applying all diligence". NASB.**

We must do something, for without action on our part, nothing will bring us to our goals or results. We must make or do simultaneously all our speed in eagerness, earnestness and dispatch toward our goals or results, as well as, perform all constant and earnest effort to accomplish what is undertaken. We must put forth actions with all effort, by exerting our mind and body, to produce and accomplish the goals and results desired. This is so, because God has already placed this ability within us to do it, through His promises.

The next phrase "add to your faith goodness", "add" is defined (S): "to furnish besides, that is fully supply, (figuratively) aid or contributes", and (Y): "to furnish abundantly", and (D): "to unite or join so as to increase the number, quantity, size or importance".

We must add to, that is, furnish besides, fully supply and aid or contribute in an abundant fashion. It is up to us to add, supply or give to each function of the fruit of the Spirit, by uniting or joining, so as to increase the number, quantity, size or importance in our lives.

The first word "faith" is defined (S): "persuasion, credence, conviction, reliance and constancy", and (Y): "faith, faithfulness, steadfastness"' Please turn back to the chapter covering faith, to better understand. Peter continues to add, until we can reach the desired goals and results. Many of these are the same as Paul calls the fruit of the Spirit.

The next word "goodness" is defined (S): "manliness (valor), that is excellence (intrinsic= belonging to a thing by its very nature), (attributed= to regard as resulting from, considered as caused by)", and (Y): "force or strength (of mind or body)", and (D): "moral excellence; righteousness; conformity of one's life and conduct to moral and ethical principles; inherent power to produce effects; potency". **Alternate versions: "virtue" KJV, "moral excellence" NASB, and "virtue (excellence, resolution, Christian energy)" AMP.**

Goodness is the active doing of good, that is the manliness, valor and excellence in its very nature that belongs to it, and caused by or resulting from itself. When we continually act on being good, it will develop into goodness by its very nature, caused by and resulting from doing good. Please turn back to the chapter on goodness, to get a better understanding.

The following word "knowledge" is defined (S): "knowing (the act), that is (by implication) knowledge", and (D): "acquaintance with facts,

Temperance: the eighth step on the foundation of love

truths or principles, as from study or investigation; fact or state of knowing; perception of fact or truth; clear and certain apprehension".

Knowledge acquaints us with facts, truths and principles, and is obtained by us from studying and investigation. The more knowledge we have, the greater perception, clarity and certainty of mental apprehension we will have. When we decide to accept and receive the redemptive work of Jesus on the cross for ourselves, we are recreated with eternal life from God. Therefore, as born again/recreated believers, we must use our minds more effectively and not disregard it as evil. God never said not to use our minds, but to line them up to God's word and way; found in **Romans 12:2: "Do not conform any longer to the pattern of this world, but be transformed by the renewing of your mind. Then you will be able to test and approve what God's will is—his good, pleasing and perfect will". NIV.** It is our responsibility to study and investigate God's word, as well as, acquire knowledge man has discovered. Worldly knowledge is not evil in itself, but the use of it determines the quality, whether it's good or evil.

Self-control comes after knowledge, which was described earlier in this chapter. We, many times, try to be temperate/self-controlled, without the necessary tools to ensure success. When we fail, we just give up, not knowing that all we need is some tools properly used. When we decide to act temperate/self-controlled, yet feel inadequate to do so, we must remember that we need preparation with the proper tools of faith, goodness and knowledge first.

The next word *"perseverance"* is defined (S): *"cheerful (or hopeful) endurance, constancy"*, and (Y): *"endurance, continuance"*, and (D): *"the bearing of provocation, annoyance, misfortune, pain, etc., without complaint, loss of temper, irritation or the like; quiet perseverance; even-tempered care; diligence"*.

There are similarities with longsuffering, yet it is the position that differs. It is us towards others that determines the results in longsuffering, while it is others towards us that determines the results in perseverance. Both require from us to be in endurance or constancy. Longsuffering shows how we endure or persevere, and react to others when they are challenged, while perseverance shows how we endure or persevere, and react to ourselves when we are challenged. We now can persevere, in conjunction with faith, goodness and knowledge, because we are prepared in advance knowing that whatever the circumstance, we can go through no matter how long it takes. We can bear provocation, annoyance, misfortune, pain, etc., without complaining, loss of temper, irritation or the like, being in even-tempered care.

"Godliness" is defined (S): *"piety, specifically the gospel theme"*, and (Y): *"piety, reverence"*, and (D): *conforming to the laws and wish-*

es of God; devout; pious (reverence for God or devout fulfillment of religious obligations; holiness".

Once we obtain faith, goodness, knowledge, self-control and perseverance, then godliness puts us into a realm where there is responsibility. This action of godliness/ holiness must demonstrate the gospel theme (good news). We are to conform to the laws and wishes of God (God's word), by being reverent to God or devout in fulfilling our religious obligations. **(James 1:27 states: "Religion that God our Father accepts as pure and faultless is this: to look after orphans and widows in their distress and to keep oneself from being polluted by the world". NIV.).** Whatever God asks us to do, He always provides the way and the tools needed to accomplish them. What we must do is first find out about them, then learn how they function, followed by acting on them to receive the benefits. If we decide not to act on them, we are still responsible for them. We must always strive to get better, therefore we have no excuse for not having, knowing or refusing to learn, thinking we won't be responsible.

Godliness/holiness is God's requirement from us. Here are some Scriptures to back up this claim. **I Peter 1:16: "...it is written, 'you shall be holy, for I am holy'". NAS. Titus 1:1b: "...the knowledge of the truth which is according to godliness". NAS. I Timothy 2:1-2: "...that requests, prayers, intercession and thanksgiving be made for everyone...that we may live peaceful and quiet lives in all godliness and holiness". NIV. I Timothy 4;7b-8: "...discipline yourself for the purpose of godliness; for bodily discipline is only of little profit, but godliness is profitable for all things, since it holds promise for the present life and also for the life to come". NAS.** Godliness involves our diligence to be effective. **2 Timothy 2:15: "Be diligent to present yourself approved to God as a workman who does not need to be ashamed, handling accurately the word of truth". NAS.**

"Brotherly kindness", in Greek is "philadelphia", is defined (S): "fraternal affection", and (Y): "love of the brotherhood", and (D): "the state or quality of a good or benevolent nature or disposition; indulgent, considerate or helpful".

Brotherly kindness and gentleness are similar in character. Gentleness is described as usefulness and having moral excellence in character or demeanor, often suggesting a deliberate or voluntary kindness in dealing with others. It is a willingness to do good or give pleasure, and a deep-seated characteristic shown by considerate behavior. Brotherly kindness is a fraternal affection/kindness, a love for the brotherhood, and is the state or quality of a good or benevolent nature or dis-

Temperance: the eighth step on the foundation of love

position to a brother, being indulgent, considerate and helpful. The difference is that gentleness is directed to others outside the camp of believers, while brotherly kindness is directed to those within the camp of believers. It is the same quality, but it reaches out to different classes of people. Some Scriptures on brotherly love: **Romans 12:10a: "Be devoted to one another in brotherly love". NIV. I Peter 1:22: "Since you have in obedience to the truth purified your souls for a sincere love of the brethren, fervently love one another from the heart..."**. NAS. **Hebrews 13:1: "Keep on loving each other as brothers". NIV.**

"Love" is defined (S): "love, that is affection or benevolence; specifically (plural) a love-feast". We have extensively covered "charity/love" in a previous chapter. Please go back to refresh your understanding.

Peter, here, has led us back to the foundation of the fruit of the Spirit. No matter the previous order, it must always lead back to the foundation or principle called love. Love is the key to any and all actions in life, since it is the initial building block God has set up. Love willingly gives to another, therefore it can reach out from itself through any other function of the fruit of the Spirit. We must decide ultimately, to operate in love, then any and all of the other functions of the fruit of the Spirit will work properly and efficiently.

The word "ineffective" is defined (S): "inactive, that is unemployed; (by implication) lazy, useless", and (Y): "not working", and (D): "not producing or incapable of producing offspring; unproductive; unfruitful; without capacity to interest or attract; mentally unproductive; dull; stupid; not producing results".

Verse 8 of II Peter 1 states: "For if you possess these qualities in increasing measure, they will keep you from being ineffective and unproductive in your knowledge of our Lord Jesus Christ". When we are actively involved in the fruit of the Spirit, then it is impossible to be inactive, unemployed, lazy and useless. Matthew 20:3,6 shows us the landowner found idle men and put them to work in his vineyard, therefore we must put ourselves to work to produce. If we are active in the fruit of the Spirit, we will not be unproductive/ unfruitful. Therefore, we will not be without capacity to interest or attract the knowledge of the Lord Jesus Christ, or be mentally unproductive, dull or stupid, not producing results. The knowledge of our Lord Jesus Christ comes only when we decide to accept and receive the redemptive work of Jesus. God wants to lavish all good on us, yet He doesn't waste it on unbelievers who constantly resist Him. Why not come over to the winning side?

We see, in verse 9 of II Peter 1, when we are inactive in the fruit of the Spirit, we are essentially blind or near-sighted. We, in this condition, quickly forget that we have been cleansed from our past sins. God never wants us burdened down by sins past, present or future, because Jesus already paid the ultimate price so we do not have to.

The phrase, in verse 10 of II Peter 1, opens a new command or mandate from previous information: "...be all the more eager to make...". When we receive and apprehend new information/revelation from God's word and promises, we must act on it immediately to make it sure in our lives. **Hebrews 2:1-3 states: the message spoken by angels was binding/proved unalterable, therefore we must not ignore/neglect it when we hear it. II Peter 1:19 states: the word of prophecy is more certain/sure: which lights up within our hearts, revealed. Hebrews 3:14 states: we must hold on to the confidence/assurance we get through His word until the end, when we see the word of God in action in our lives, keeping our hearts sensitive. NIV/NASB.**

The phrase "you will never fall" is the result. The word "fall" is defined (S): "to trip, that is (figuratively) to err, fail (of salvation)", and (Y): "to stumble", and (D): "to become of a lower level, degree, amount, quality, value, number, etc.; to succumb to temptation, especially to become unchaste or to lose one's innocence; to lose status, position, dignity, character, etc.". A commentary: "to make a false step or mistake, to fail". DAKES.

What a promise! If we decide, not God or anyone else, to do all God has required of us, we will never fail/stumble, ever. We will never succumb to temptation and become unchaste, whether in spirit, soul or body, nor lose our status, position, dignity and character, nor make a false step or mistake, or fail. We must not deviate from temperance, yet it will not work without action. It must be accompanied with action to function, or else it is dead, just like faith, love, longsuffering, etc.

James 3:2 states: "If anyone is never at fault in what he says, he is a perfect man able to keep his whole body in check". NIV. This can happen only when we are totally in tune to God's word. We know that God's word never fails, so we must conclude that when we operate fully within the word, we also will never fail.

Now let's summarize on the subject of temperance. We found that temperance involves our direct action of self-control, for our flesh bodies are ever trying to take control. God placed in us temperance, but we must develop it, where we will be able to control the natural appetites or passions that causes over-indulgence.

Temperance must be strived for by setting the appropriate goals to obtain the results desired, and pressure must be put on, by strict training for the results to come about. We must put pressure on our flesh bodies

Temperance: the eighth step on the foundation of love

to gain control and victory, where we can, by this strict training, regulate the flesh body to do what it was designed to do. Once developed properly, we won't need to struggle needlessly for our trained flesh body will not dominate.

We must take the first step by putting forth action to accomplish the goal, and this can be done since God already gave us the ability. All we need to do is exercise it, which starts with the first move on our part.

Temperance is not the first thing we strive for, for we must have a foundation first. We found in I Peter 1:5-10, that faith, goodness and knowledge must be in place first for temperance/self-control to function properly, and ensure its success. If we are failing, or not getting the results we really desire, we must remember that preparation with the proper tools of faith, goodness and knowledge will set us on track.

There is action with all the fruit of the Spirit, which puts us in a responsible position. All this is put on the foundation of love, the initial building block God has set up. Any and all functions of the fruit of the Spirit will work properly by love. We, without action, will be ineffective/useless and unproductive/unfruitful, and considered blind and nearsighted, where we forget our true position as born-again believers. Jesus already paid the price for our sins, therefore we do not have to sin by our inaction.

Any new information/revelation we receive or apprehend from God's word, we must act on it immediately, where it becomes sure and real to us. If we do not neglect it in our lives, we will gain surety/confidence, as we see God's word in action in our lives.

When WE decide to do all the functions of the fruit of the Spirit, WE WILL NOT FALL, EVER. We won't succumb to temptation, since our flesh body is under control by temperance. We will keep our status, position, dignity, character, etc., and not make a false step, mistake or fail.

We see that temperance originates in our spirit man, but functions through our flesh body, just like faith and meekness. Temperance controls our flesh body from over-indulging and causing it to dominate. When our flesh body is under control, it can then function properly as God designed it to be. We won't succumb to temptation, but overcome them victoriously, having our flesh body doing the word of God and not the word of over-indulgence.

Faith operates through our flesh, since faith without action is dead, therefore faith with action is alive to faithfulness. Meekness operates through our flesh to submit to God's word, moving us to the right result goals, as God intended for our good and benefit. Temperance operates through our flesh by controlling the over-indulgence, so we won't succumb to them, but leading us to victory.

12

Conclusion and Summary

We have come to the end of our survey on the fruit of the Spirit, and it is in no way exhausting the subject, but only an introduction to what we have received from God when we become born-again believers. Once we know what we have received, we need to put it into practice, or else, we will never receive the benefits. If we have $1 million in our bank account, yet never exercise our rights to use it, we obtain no benefit from having it. Therefore, the fruit of the Spirit, which was placed in our spirit man when we were born-again, will not benefit us if we do not exercise our right to use it. We may say, "We do not know how?" Well, God doesn't give us something without showing us how to use it properly to obtain the most from it. A car manufacturer doesn't sell a car and not give a manual on how to take care of it to obtain maximum use from it=satisfied customer. God also gives us the principles to take care of the fruit of the Spirit within us, to obtain the maximum use from it=satisfied believer.

We will briefly review the nine functions of the fruit of the Spirit, which include: love, joy, peace, longsuffering, gentleness, goodness, faith, meekness and temperance. Each function depends on the other, and they are accumulative.

The first function is called love, from the Greek word agape, meaning benevolence. This is the willful giving of ourselves to another to meet their real need. It also means affection, which is the heart love for another. God's love is not natural fleshly love, which is only temporary and is greatly affected by circumstances and situations in life. God's kind of love is always steadfast, and is the foundation, standard or principle function of the fruit of the Spirit.

The second function is called joy, which is not an emotional feeling only, but a strength that comes by a fortified place or defense. Joy gives us the ability to celebrate and fills us to capacity, and it cannot be taken from us unless we decide to let it go. It is orderly and steadfast, therefore reliable, and must be based on the foundation of love, where joy can enrich us with strength as our defense.

The third function is called peace, and it is not the lack of war or disputes as the world sees it. Peace was given, and sent forth for us by Jesus. We need not be in fear of any trouble with this peace and must hold onto it to prevent loss to the enemy. We must not submit to tribulations against us, since Jesus already defeated the enemy, Satan. Peace equals quiet assurance that keeps, guards and protects us in our hearts and minds, where we can have prosperity and success. Peace with authority gives us continual victory as an offense. Jesus settled the dispute between God and Satan, therefore peace must rule in our hearts or arbitrate, and be the most important influence and persuasion of its success.

The first three functions of love, joy and peace operates from our spirit man, and these cause us to be like God. We, in love, become true givers, in joy, become strengthened, and in peace, become fighters against the enemy.

The fourth function is called longsuffering, and it is the patient endurance of hardships and injuries without reacting. It chooses not to flare up, but waits before action is taken, because it looks for a way to appease and calm down. It has great understanding to acquire intelligence, where we can reason with the intent to persuade or convince by yielding, in an effort to break down the distrust and hostility. It takes into account and leads our minds with official authority, so that we can receive from God. It's not pushy or demanding, and doesn't lash out at others faults and errors. Lastly, it is worn as clothing so others can see and desire the same, and it is considered a great act with a setting of praise and testimony.

The fifth function is called gentleness, and it is useful by being morally excellent in character or demeanor. It remains faithful to God no matter what the situation, and doesn't fight against but trusts God's deliverance. It draws us near to each other, and not apart by quarrels or disputes, in turn we become easy to talk to, friendly and show warmth, thereby pulling down walls where we can reach out to help, by being pliable, considerate and yielding to the needs of others. We can, in God's wisdom, operate in gentleness, for it ensures us to be appropriate and considerate.

The sixth function is called goodness, and it is moral excellence in active goodness being God-like in life and conduct. It has the inherent power to produce effects with potency and it is in pursuit to overcome us to fill our lives. God hid it for us and not from us, for it was laid up abundantly with care, embellished and beautifully ornamented, and bestowed upon us to apply. We must be desirous to be satisfied, where the end of our needs, desires and wants are met sufficiently or amply supplied, so that we can share with others who don't know about God's goodness. It has great value or riches for our use and enjoyment when we rely totally on God even when we are abundantly supplied. Goodness leads us to repentance, not self-abasement, by being humble before God and turning away from sin.

The second three functions of the fruit of the Spirit covers our soul part of man (will, emotion and intellect). These give us the ability to stabilize and control our soul to think in line with God's word and will, see God work in our lives to understand others, and how to minister to them what God has given them.

The seventh function is called faith, and it is a persuasion, credence, moral conviction, reliance and constancy. Faith accompanied by actions produce faithfulness. Faith has the title deed of ownership, because faith has substance and it is not inanimate. When we take ownership, by exercising to develop quality, we will become faithful to it. Faith must be spoken out from prepared and preplanned end results desired from God's word. Faith must be used by us voluntarily, for it will not fall on us or force itself on us. Words are containers having within them the directives, faith and anointing.

The eighth function is called meekness, by implication, humility, which has great fortitude and brings great exaltation from God. Meekness is not self-degradation but submission to God to move on our behalf by putting aside our ways, and submitting to God's ways, who provides guidance. Meekness teaches us to go on roads trodden, proven for our good, where we have authority to take our rightful inheritance, and bring about abundance with delight. Meekness controls us from being provoked by others, while quietness controls us from being provoking to others.

The ninth function is called temperance, It is our direct action of self-control, resulting in us controlling our natural appetites or passions from over-indulgence. We must strive for temperance, putting pressure on it for the results to come about, the control of our flesh body. We must take the first step to start, for God already placed within us temperance to use. Temperance without a strong foundation, like faith, goodness and knowledge, will not work properly and ultimately will not succeed.

The third three functions cover our flesh part of man. Faith, with action, comes alive to faithfulness. Meekness, with action, comes to submit to God's way for our good and benefit, moving us to the right result goals. Temperance, with action, comes to control our fleshly over-indulgence, where we won't succumb to it, but leading us to victory.

We must realize that these functions of the fruit of the Spirit are useful only for the believers. If believers have trouble operating in these,

Conclusion and Summary

imagine how impossible it is for unbelievers! These functions are only compatible to the believers. If we try to do these on our own, without being a believer, all our efforts are futile. We must decide to become a believer, where at that moment, these functions are placed within us.

It may be said, "Why become a believer?". The Bible explains why, since it is the ultimate source for life.

The first reason is that God loves us! John 3:16 states: "For God so loved the world, that He gave His only begotten Son, that whoever believes in Him should not perish, but have eternal life". NAS. Romans 5:8 states: "But God demonstrates His own love toward us, in that while we were yet sinners, Christ died for us". NAS.

The second reason is that we are all sinners. Romans 3:23 states: "...for all have sinned and fall short of the glory of God,". NAS. Romans 3:10 states: "...as it is written, 'There is none righteous, not even one;". NAS.

The third reason is that God has provided redemption for all. Romans 6:23 states: "For the wages of sin is death, but the free gift of God is eternal life in Christ Jesus our Lord". NAS. John 1:12 states: "But as many as received Him, to them He gave the right to become children of God, even to those who believe in His name,". NAS.

The fourth reason is that we all need to be saved now. Revelation 3:20 states: "Behold, I stand at the door and knock; if anyone hears My voice and opens the door, I will come in to him, and will dine with him, and he with Me". NAS. Romans 10:13 states: "...for 'Whoever will call upon the name of the Lord will be saved'". NAS. II Corinthians 6:2 states: "...for He says, 'At the acceptable time I listened to you, and on the day of salvation I helped you'; behold, now is 'The acceptable time', behold, now is 'The day of salvation...'". NAS. Romans 10:9-10 states: "...that if you confess with your mouth Jesus as Lord, and believe in your heart that God raised Him from the dead, you shall be saved; for with the heart man believes, resulting in righteousness, and with the mouth he confesses, resulting in salvation". NAS.

If we are serious about living for God and not for ourselves, let's take the first step. Please repeat this model prayer out loud and believe it with the heart.

"Dear God. I am coming to You as I am. I cannot change myself. My sins keep me from You, but You, Father, have provided for me the Savior, Jesus. I now decide to believe and receive the redemptive work of Jesus on the cross for me. Therefore, I now confess with my mouth "Jesus is Lord of my life", and I now believe it with my heart. Thank-You Jesus for dying for my sins and rising from the dead to bring me life. Therefore, my sins are forgiven and I am now a believer. I am now set free from sin and choose to follow you. Thank-You in Jesus' name. Amen"

Now that we have done the first and most important step in our lives, we now have the fruit of the Spirit within our spirit man. We must start acting on it, where we can commence on developing and making the fruit of the Spirit a reality in our lives. It will feel awkward at first, but with continual practice, it will become habitual to us, where we will not struggle in doing it.

For any and all information, please write to:
By the Cross and Beyond Ministries.
P.O. Box 1062
Cadillac, Michigan 49601